Why On Earth Did God Let This Happen... For Heaven's Sake?

Dr. Kent Hovind

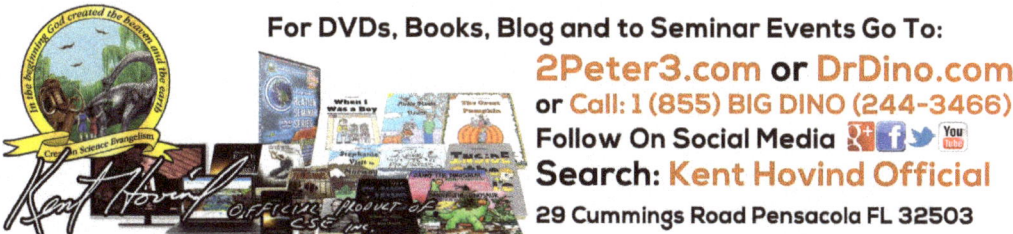

For DVDs, Books, Blog and to Seminar Events Go To:
2Peter3.com or **DrDino.com**
or Call: 1 (855) BIG DINO (244-3466)
Follow On Social Media
Search: Kent Hovind Official
29 Cummings Road Pensacola FL 32503

All Scripture quotations, unless otherwise indicated, are taken from King James Version. Hyperlinks for eBook provided by http://www.kingjamesbibleonline.org/.

Creation Science Evangelism, Inc.
Copyright © 2013 Kent Hovind All Rights Reserved. Published 2013
ISBN HARDBACK 978-1-944010-29-4
ISBN EBOOK 978-1-944010-04-1
Written by Dr. Kent Hovind
29 Cummings RD Pensacola FL 32503 (855) BIG DINO (244-3466) 2Peter3.com DrDino.com

Printed in the United States of America
Distributed by Creation Science Evangelism, Inc.
For more information visit drdino.com or 2peter3.com

Table of Contents

Introduction 5
Dear God Kneemail Book 1: November 2006 – December 2007
- John the Baptist 8
- Phillip 10
- Joseph 11
- Cain 12
- Abel 13
- Shem 15
- Bildad and Job 17
- Moses 20
- Job 21
- The Castle, The Bishop and Master 23
- David and Eliab 25
- The Potter's Vase 27
- Still Waiting on God 29
- Mrs. Job 31
- Mordecai 33
- Martha 34
- The Mission Field in G20 35
- Another New Field Part 1 37
- Another New Field Part 2 38
- Church in G20 39
- Why Suffering 41
- Prince Malchiah 43
- Potiphar 45
- Noah 46
- The Ax and the Woodsman 47
- The Woodsman to the Ax 48
- Urbane 50
- Peter 51
- Ebed-melech 52
- The Order of the Arrow 55
- Daniel 59
- A Few Questions 60
- Simon the Zealot 70
- Psalm 23 and Numbers 73
- How Much Longer? 76
- Naboth 83
- A Day in the Prison Life 88
- Pay Attention Son! 92
- Kent 2007, Kent 2011 and Moses 96
- Reflections on Job's Suffering and Christian Trials 100
- Elijah's Proclamation for "No Rain" 103

Joseph's Prison Sentence	108
Ship Captain to Italy and Passenger, Apostle Paul	112
Ship Captain to Alexandria	114
Discussion with Hitler on Equating Humans with Animals	115
A Young Man's Decision – A True Story	118
Give me Wisdom	121
Hidden Sin and Forgiveness	123
Pressure	129
Luther Bridges 'A Song Born in Tragedy'	133
Widow Woman on God's Provision	135
Essay on John Bunyan's Trial	137
God and the Young Boy – Caterpillar Power Parade	141
Motives for Reading the Word of God	144
Goliath of Gath – Only the Strongest Survive	146
Lazarus' Resurrection	150
Bidkar on Wicked Queen Jezebel	152
Apostle Paul on Prison Encouragement and Discouragement	154
Forgiveness	159
Hur on FANAFI	163
Discouragement - Satan's Favorite Tool!	166
Jacob, Why Are You Still in Egypt?	175
Azor on Loving Earthly Wealth	178
Young Father – Walking with God; Family Devotions	182
Malchus	185
All Call – Oh No! Now What?	188
A Soldier Enlisted – For the Duration	192
Gaddi – Disobedience, Distrust, Anger and Murder	194
Zimri and Cozbi	197
Colonel Sanford – The Love of Money	199
Kent and Scientist on the Living Word – Help! It's Hot!	203
One More Night with the Frogs	205
What a Gift!	207
Four Hundred Days	209
Michal, Saul's Daughter, on Bitterness	211
Questions From the Biology Textbook	215
Ahithophel	219
End of the Year Update	223

Introduction

DEAR GOD...

This book is a result of a tragedy that God used for good, as He always does, combined with my hyperactive and slightly eccentric mind.

Jesus told a lot of classic stories that immediately bring a picture to your mind. Matthew 7:3-5 is one of my favorites.

> "³And why beholdest thou the mote that is in thy brother's eye, but considerest not the beam that is in thine own eye? ⁴Or how wilt thou say to thy brother, Let me pull out the mote out of thine eye; and, behold, a beam is in thine own eye? ⁵Thou hypocrite, first cast out the beam out of thine own eye; and then shalt thou see clearly to cast out the mote out of thy brother's eye."

As you read it, you immediately imagine yourself watching a man with a log stuck in his eye bending over helping a friend get a speck out of his!

Jesus often told stories or asked questions to make His audience stop and think long and hard and to teach life-changing truths. Many times, the questions are never answered. God asked Job eighty-four questions—none of which were answered, but those questions sure made Job think! He repented at the end just because of God's questions! The book of Jonah ends with a question that is never answered.

Over my many years of ministry for the Lord, I have been in scores of situations that have made me stop and think. This book contains imaginary letters from my hyperactive mind. I have left them in the order that they were written. These "snapshots" of my life and the lives of various others are designed to make you "selah"—stop and think (Psalm 3:2). Any resemblance between these writings and a real book is purely coincidental.

There is no particular plot or theme to this book. It is rather a collection of my random musings as I rode the emotional roller coaster that anyone locked away from their loved ones clearly understands. Often, during my own Bible reading time, I would come across a Bible character and decide to "knee-mail" them. I had a wonderful time "talking" with these people and I learned a lot from them.

I gave my life to Jesus Christ at age sixteen on February 9, 1969. I have been trying to serve God since then. After teaching high school science and math for fifteen years, God led me to start Creation Science Evangelism in 1989. This ministry defends the Bible as being scientifically accurate and exposes evolution as being the dumbest and most dangerous religion in the history of humanity. Our goal has always been to bring people to Christ and strengthen the faith of believers.

After a long and frustrating battle with the IRS, I was sent to prison on November 2, 2006 to serve a ten-year sentence for alleged violation of IRS codes in relation to our church ministry. Prayerfully, the case will be overturned and our ministry exonerated of all charges (see freekenthovind.com for details). It was during my first twelve months of incarceration that this book was written.

It started because I was simply writing updates on my status from the county jail for our ministry blog site, kenthovindblog.com. Interspersed with these were the first "Dear God letters," as I called them. In May of 2007, I began writing to God and getting "His response" in the form of "E-Mails". It was suggested I call them "Knee-Mails" instead—most appropriate.

Some have suggested that many of these writings can be used as mini-dramas before church services, in Sunday school classes, etc. Persons in the dramas could dress in character and the part of God could be read offstage via the sound system. It may sometimes be helpful to summarize the Bible story, or read the actual Scripture before the drama.

These letters may also be sent to encourage those who are suffering, are lonely, or who question God. There are millions of people who would be encouraged just to receive a letter. There are over two million people who are in jail or prison in America, the largest per capita of any country in the world. Many of these people never get any mail and would be encouraged to get a brief letter with a tract or one of these "Dear God" letters. You can ask a jail chaplain for a list of inmates that never receive mail.

There are many others in nursing homes, hospitals, or serving in the military or on mission fields that could benefit from a letter. If every Christian would pick three to five people to pray for each week and to visit or write each week, we could help "bear one another's burdens, and so fulfill the law of Christ" (Galatians 6:2).

It is my prayer that these letters will bless you, inspire you to lead others to a relationship with their Creator, draw you closer to Christ, and strengthen your faith. Especially to those in prison—may God bless you. I truly know how you feel. I "sat where you sat" (Ezekiel 3:15). Use your prison time to grow closer to God. Talk to Him. He loves you!

May all glory, praise, and honor go to Him!

Kent Hovind

LETTER FROM GOD TO JOHN THE BAPTIST
November 2006
(written from Escambia County Jail - based on Matthew 14:3; Mark 6:17; Luke 3:20)

Dear John the Baptist,

I am sorry to hear that you are in prison; and I hate to say it, but I warned you that this would happen. When I heard you preach in the wilderness, I was amazed at the power of God on your ministry. I was there with thousands of others listening to you preach. It was so exciting that even now—years later—I get goose bumps when I recall those great sermons and those huge crowds.

You may not remember me; but after you baptized me in Jordan, you invited me to join you for lunch. I was so honored to be able to sit with you and a few of your disciples, that I really did not mind eating locust and wild honey. I loved listening to you discussing issues facing our nation with your disciples. I didn't say much, but when you were discussing how Herod had broken both God's law and man's law by marrying Herodias, his brother Philip's wife, I said, "Mr. Baptist, I think you have an awesome ministry preaching repentance, but your meddling in politics will get you in trouble."

You said, "Son, God has called me to preach His truth to all, including politicians. They need a voice crying out to them also. My job is to obey God and preach the truth. God's men are required to reprove, rebuke, and exhort. It does not matter if we are preaching to servants or kings."

I said, "You must do what you think is right. But I have a strong feeling that meddling in politics will result in trouble." We finished dinner and you went back to preaching, and I went home to get back to work.

And now it has happened: you are in jail. I am still a believer and follow Jesus as you told your disciples to do. But, I have a few questions. Can you help me with these questions, as I have searched the Scriptures and my soul and cannot find an answer? There is no question about Herod's being wrong in doing what he did. There is no question that you were right in what you said. But my questions are these:

1. Do you still think you did the wise thing in rebuking and thus provoking Herod?
2. Should Christians get involved in political issues like you did, or just preach the Gospel?
3. Is it right for Christians to be involved in revolutions against tyrants and wicked kings who oppress their people?
4. Since Jesus said, "Verily I say unto you among them that are born of women there has not risen greater than John the Baptist," (Matthew 11:11) why are you in jail?

Your perplexed young friend,
Andrew (John 1:40)

My challenge to all Christians: Please write a paragraph explaining what you believe about John the Baptist. Was he wise or foolish to rebuke Herod?

WRITTEN THROUGH PHILIP'S EYES FROM THE BOOK OF ACTS
December 22, 2006
(after learning that Judge Rodgers denied our motion for release)

Dear God,

I hate to complain but... I was busy leading a great revival in Samaria (Acts 8:5-25) in which thousands were being saved; demons were being cast out; sick were being healed; the entire land of Samaria was seeing revival; and I was happy and busy serving You and winning souls. Now I am standing in the Gaza Desert! There is nobody here, Lord—no crowds to minister to. Do You know what You are doing, Lord?

Yes, Lord, I see that chariot coming. But look, Lord. It's only one man and his skin color does not match mine. He's black. He looks like a foreign officer. Surely You did not bring me all the way down here to witness to one man from another country. This man, even if he trusts You, God, will never bear any fruit for Your Kingdom.

Why did You take me away from my revival ministry where thousands were being saved to witness to one insignificant man? Lord, I don't understand, and I would sure rather be home with my four daughters that also witness for You (Acts 21:9). However, since You brought me here, I will go talk to this man. I sure hope You know what you're doing! We'll talk about this later, Lord.

"Hey there, you, driving the chariot, may I come talk with you?"

Obeying but Discouraged,
Philip

PS Little did Philip realize that this Ethiopian eunuch would go back to his country and lead probably one of the greatest revivals in history. By the time other Christians arrived in Ethiopia sometime later, there were already tens of thousands of believers, because of this new convert in the Gaza Desert. The church today still thrives in Ethiopia—two thousand years later!

WRITTEN THROUGH JOSEPH'S EYES FROM THE BOOK OF GENESIS
December 29, 2006

Dear God,

This is Joseph, and we need to talk. I'm not real happy with the way You are managing Your world, and especially with what You have allowed to happen to me. I was my Dad's favorite child (Genesis 37:3), and things were going fine. I had a nice place to live. I had a great family with ten brothers. Then You started giving me dreams (Genesis 37:5,9) about them bowing to me, and my world fell apart. They hated me and would have killed me if Reuben had not rescued me (Genesis 37:21).

Then I was sold as a slave and ended up in Egypt. The next thing I knew, I was promoted to be a well-respected head of all Potiphar's household. Life was looking up again! Then Potiphar's wife tried to seduce me (Genesis 39:2). Lord, I did what was right. I obeyed Your laws. I ran out of the house. What should I have done? Then I was thrown in prison for doing right! Why am I in prison? Lord, it just doesn't seem fair. Why would You let this happen to me? I am trying to serve You, God. Are You even listening?

Yes, I see the King's butler and baker over there looking scared (Genesis 40:1). But God, what about me? Okay, God, I will go talk to them, but I still need some answers. I will get back to You later...

Obeying but with questions,
Joseph

PS: Joseph remained faithful to God and did not justify himself. He did not know it at the time, but God was about to exalt him to the position of Vice-Pharaoh of Egypt, the greatest kingdom on earth at the time. God would use Joseph to save his entire family and change world history!

WRITTEN THROUGH THE EYES OF CAIN TO GOD
January 2, 2007
(written during a time of deep discouragement for all people locked up over the holidays)

Dear God,

I think You made a huge mistake. Yesterday, I was feeling grateful for the nice world you made and I wanted to show my appreciation by bringing You a sacrifice. I had worked hard in my garden all summer to raise beautiful fruits and vegetables, just for this day. And You didn't even take notice! You could have at least said something!

I know that You are busy and all, but ignoring me hurt my feelings, God, a lot! When I was little, I would color pictures for Mom and Dad. They weren't real good, but they showed my heart. My parents always made me feel special for trying. Mom was especially good at encouraging me. She would say to Adam, "Honey, look what Cain drew for us. Isn't it beautiful?"

God, I know You made the world and all, but You could learn a few things about how to treat people from my Mom! You hurt my feelings, God. It hurt even more when You made such a big deal out of my brother's offering. I can't believe that You would get some kind of sick enjoyment out of seeing an innocent lamb killed and burned up. Abel didn't work for his gift at all. I worked all summer. I get mad every time I think about it. I still think You made a mistake, God. You need to think about it one more time.

There goes Abel now. I'll go talk to him about it, too. I know I can change his mind if he will listen...

WRITTEN THROUGH THE EYES OF ABEL TO GOD
January 2, 2007

Dear God,

I don't understand what happened. Dad told us all about the Garden of Eden before he and Mom sinned. From what Dad says, it was an incredible place. He also told us how You had to kill a lamb for their sins. Dad explained how if we ever brought a sacrifice to you, it had to be a lamb. So that is what I did.

My brother Cain worked hard to raise the best fruits and vegetables to bring to You. Yet You rejected his offering. I think I understand why. But what I don't understand is, why he is mad at me. I did what You said, Lord. Cain is my brother, Lord. It doesn't make sense that he would want to hurt me over this. He sure seems to be upset. Well, here he comes...

I will try to talk to him one more time. We need to talk later, God.

Hey Cain! How are you doing?...

Little did Abel realize that he would be the first of many millions who would suffer death in the great war between the only two religions on planet earth. The "do" religion, and the "done" religion. The "do" people, like Cain, believe that God will accept them based on what they do to please Him. While the items on the list may vary from group to group, a "do list" remains. The "done religion" people, like Able, know that God accepts them based on what is done by an innocent substitute.

Are you trusting your works to go to Heaven, or are you trusting Jesus Christ and the cross of Calvary?

Why On Earth Did God Let This Happen... For Heaven's Sake?

WRITTEN THROUGH THE EYES OF SHEM TO GOD
January 2, 2007

Dear God,

God, we need to talk. I am trying to be a good son. But this time my dad has gone too far! He claims that You told him to build this giant boat in the middle of our field. God, listen! All my friends at school are laughing at me for being part of this crazy family. No one wants to be seen with me, and I never get invited to anything. I guess it is just as well, since all we do is work on that dumb boat from sunrise to sunset. Lord, I just want to have a normal life. You know—get married, build a house, and raise the kids. What is wrong with that? Isn't that the way You designed this world? Isn't that normal?

Why do we have to be the oddballs? How does Dad think that he is going to get that boat moved to the water anyway? This whole idea seems silly, Lord! How am I supposed to know that You told Dad to do this? Why don't You show me a vision, God? Japheth says that he has doubts about this whole thing also, Lord. Ham told me that this project has ruined his dating life. So he just works hard to forget his problems.

I think You need to talk to Dad, God. He's doing harm to our family's reputation. "I'm coming, Dad! I know, Dad. You need a four-by-six that is six and a half cubits long. Coming right away."

We'll talk some more later, God.
Shem

WRITTEN TO BILDAD, FROM JOB
January 4, 2007

Dear Bildad,

Thank you for coming to visit me during my time of grief. I know that it was a great sacrifice in many ways for you to leave your family and travel so far to spend a few weeks with me. Thanks also, for your friendship over the years.

The first week when you were just quietly sitting with me was a great comfort. There is no way to describe the anguish of soul that I felt after losing my ten children, all of my wealth, my health, and the support of my wife. I pray it never happens to you like this. Your concern and your presence was a comfort to me.

I have a serious concern, however, about your advice during the second week. I think that you have two serious flaws in your logic that need corrected.

First, your entire speech is based on the assumption that all this happened to me because of God's judgment on some sin in my life. Though I would be the first to admit that I am a sinner and deserve God's wrath and judgment, I am sure that this is not the cause of this current trouble. Even a quick look around the neighborhood and around the world will show that the very wicked are often very prosperous, while those who sincerely seek after God often have trials, testings, and tragedies.

In a few thousand years, the gospels will be written, and you will see that Jesus, God Himself, in the form of a man, was hungry, tired, grieved, sorrowful, tormented, tortured, and racked with pain. Yet, he was totally sinless. His life alone should show you the error of your thinking.

You can also see that Abel did right—yet Cain slew him. Joseph fled from sin—yet ended up in jail. The disciples (in two thousand years) will be beaten, jailed, threatened, or persecuted over 50 times, just in the book of Acts. I am sorry, Bildad, but you are wrong to assume that evil must be a result of someone's sin.

The second flaw in your logic that I wish to point out is your assumption that you have superior advice. You think Eliphaz's vision (Job 4:12-21) grants all of you a new level of insight into God's Word. The idea that you men know my heart because Eliphaz's hair stood up is ridiculous. There have always been shallow believers who get fooled by trusting feelings rather than trusting the Word of God. See how Isaac gets the "wool pulled over his eyes" in a few hundred years, because he trusts how "he feels" rather than the Word (Genesis 27).

I think Eliphaz saw the "spook" and heard "voices in the night" because he ate too much pizza made with bad camel milk cheese. I did that once, and my hair stood up for three days.

I don't know why for sure that God let all this happen to me. But he is God, and I am man. He is too smart and too kind to let this happen to me without a good reason.

Again, your sacrifice is greatly appreciated, as is the comfort of your presence. But your advice I question and I do not find helpful. Please seek God's mind in this matter before speaking about it. Remember that we can't see people's hearts as God can. We should not assume that all this happened because of sin on my part. Maybe God will show me all the why's someday, but until then, though he slay me, yet will I serve Him.

Sincerely,
Job
Nisan 7, 2200 B.C.

WRITTEN THROUGH THE EYES OF MOSES TO GOD
January 17, 2007
(written from the Escambia County Jail after Christian brothers wrote evil of me – based on Job 1, 2 and 42)

Dear God,

Where are You (Exodus 14:12)? I did everything you said, God. I went to talk to Pharoah just like You told me. I called upon You to bring all the plagues just like You said. When You finally let us all go, I followed the pillar of cloud.

I didn't know why You led us into the Wilderness, when I knew the way to Canaan already, and I knew this was not the way. Lord, these people have all been slaves for years and have never left Egypt, so they trusted me to lead the way and get them to the Promised Land. I should have just followed the map, but I was trying to be obedient and follow the cloud like You said, Lord.

Now, here we are trapped on this beach with mountains blocking our escape to the north and to the south; the Red Sea blocking us on the east; and a very angry Pharoah with his entire army racing down the only road to get here that we just came down from the west! Lord, where are You?

Yes, Lord, I still have my staff. Okay, Lord, I will hold it over the water. What's the battle plan, Lord? We don't even have swords, Lord? Shouldn't we be getting prepared to fight or something?

Okay, Lord. I will stand still. But I don't understand You this time, Lord.
Moses

LETTER FROM GOD TO JOB
January 19, 2007
(from the Escambia County Jail after Judge Rodgers gave me a ten-year prison sentence)

Dear Job,

I heard your prayer. I know you are wondering why this happened to you. Thanks for asking me, Job, instead of cursing me. I know you are suffering terribly right now, Job. I know that Satan has taken away your family, your health, and your wealth, even though you love me and serve me faithfully. I know it hurts you, Job. I know.

I saw the Sabeans steal your herds of animals and kill your servants, Job. I saw it. I will take care of it, Job. You have done nothing wrong. It's okay. I know it hurts you that your smelly, oozing sores have caused your neighbors to banish you from the city. And I know that your own wife is asking you to curse me and die. I heard it all, Job. I heard.

I also heard everything that your friends and enemies have been saying to you, Job. I heard it all. I know your reputation has been destroyed, and everyone thinks that you must have sinned. It's okay, Job. I know that you didn't sin. Hang on to your integrity, Job. You're doing great. It is all part of my plan.

You see, Job, there is a much bigger picture that you do not understand yet. Here are a few things for you to consider.

You're a great man, Job, and your godly influence has helped dozens of people into my kingdom. But your story of suffering will help me reach millions. Man's sin brought great pain and suffering to the world, Job. And many people blame Me. Your story will show that it is Satan, not I, that does this. I want the world to see that.

It's not over yet, Job. You have not made it to chapter 42. I will fix your suffering, Job. Hang on!

1.   *I am using you, Job, to gather evidence against those involved in your suffering for judgment day. Satan will be first. I want the world to see that I am just and fair when I banish him to hell forever.*
2.   *I will use Eliphaz's story (Job 4) to help, too, Job. Some of my "shallow" children think they are more spiritual or have special connections with me because they had a "feeling or vision." Can you believe Eliphaz thinks he knows My mind because his hair stood up? Don't listen to him, Job. I'll deal with him later.*
3.   *I'm also gathering evidence on the Sabeans, Job. Lots of people think that just because they can steal things, it is OK. They think that the strongest are better; that "might makes right." I'll deal with the Sabeans, Job. I need this as evidence for their trial.*
4.   *I will also use your story to show your neighbors and friends that it is not correct to think that all suffering is a result of sin. Most people think that, Job, and it is wrong. Bad things happen to good people. Your story will help good people understand when suffering occurs in their lives.*

I hope this helps you understand what happened to you, Job. There's just one problem; I'm not going to give you this letter until you get to heaven. You will have to trust Me until then. You'll see the big picture when you get up here, Job. Keep your chin up and be strong. I am right here with you.

**Love,
God**

THE CASTLE, THE BISHOP, AND THE CHESS MASTER
January 21, 2007

Dear Castle,

I heard your conversation with the Bishop over there and thought I would give you an explanation as to why I let you be taken out of the game by the enemy. I know you are confused and let down because you can no longer be involved in the war that you were designed for and live for. I know that being on the sidelines with other "downed" chess pieces is very hard for you. I know you are all wondering what you did wrong. You think that I don't love you or don't appreciate your worth to me. Nothing is further from the truth.

If you could only see the war from My vantage point, then you would understand. For now, you just have to trust me. I know exactly what I am doing. I will win the war. I beat this enemy every time, but he keeps coming back. He never learns.

As for your part, rest assured that you did what you were designed to do without flinching. You went where I told you and when I told you every time. You stood tall even when I sent you behind enemy lines. You helped capture the enemy Bishop and Knight. Even in that dangerous place, you obeyed My every command.

I know that you can't see the big picture, but I can. I know that your sacrifice was critical to winning the war. You don't know it now, but you not only captured some of the enemy and destroyed their seemingly impenetrable defenses on the left flank; but you also protected and encouraged some of our weaker pieces and drew their queen away, exposing the real objective.

Just rest, my dear Castle. You did exactly what I wanted you to do. Your sacrifice was part of My plan from long ago. The enemy thinks that he scored a major victory today, but watch My next move carefully. The game will soon be over. We will win in just two moves. I am proud of all my pieces—those still in the battle, and those who have sacrificed their all. Castle, trust Me. Wait and watch. I always win. You have done well.

Signed,
The Master

Why On Earth Did God Let This Happen... For Heaven's Sake?

WRITTEN FROM DAVID TO ELIAB
February 1, 2007
(based on 1 Samuel 16:6-7; 17:13; 17:28-30)

Dear Big Brother Eliab,

Sorry that I made you angry earlier today. I didn't mean to. You are my oldest brother and I look up to you in many ways. You taught me so many things growing up. I can never repay you or thank you enough.

I also want to thank you for joining Saul's army to defend our nation against the Philistines. I know you men risk your lives every day for my freedom and safety. Thank you so much. I pray for you every night as I lie out under the stars with the sheep.

Looking back on today, it seems like a dream in fast motion. I came to give you some food from Dad, heard Goliath curse God, killed him; and then you soldiers all won a great victory over our enemies. God was so good to all of us today.

There is still one unsettled issue however. After you got angry with me this morning, I asked you two questions that you did not answer (I Samuel 17:29). Please do not be angry with me. I still really want an answer to these questions.

I asked you first, "What have I done?" And second, "Is there not a cause?" I honestly would like an answer when you get time. I asked the first question because I sincerely want to be right with God. If I have done something wrong, I want to know what it was, so that I can repent. I spend lots of time talking with God and writing songs for Him as I watch the sheep. My relationship to Him means more to me than anything. Please tell me my sin so that I can confess it and forsake it.

I asked the second question, because I am just a teenager seeking the meaning of life. And you are not only my oldest brother, but also a man I deeply respect and admire. You are tall and handsome (I Samuel 16:6-7) and seem to have everything going for you; whereas, I am short and red headed (I Samuel 16:12) with lots to learn. I really want to know what "causes" people live for. I see so many causes out there. Which one is the most important?

Some of the neighbor shepherd boys love to sling stones like I do. But it seems to have consumed them. They set bowls up on the fence and try to knock them off from fifty cubits away. They are really good at it! They even have a big contest every year to see who can knock off the most bowls. They call it "Super Bowl Sabbath." Whoever wins gets a gold ring to wear. I admit, I like slinging stones, but is knocking a bowl down with a rock a good cause to live and die for?

Other boys here are consumed with racing chariots. They spend all their spare time and money working on their chariots for the races they have every Sabbath day. Some even spend two months wages just to buy gold-plated wheels. The chariots do not go faster, but more people look at them. One boy paid four hundred shekels to buy special rims that keep spinning after his chariot stops moving. Why? Is getting people's attention or going fast a cause to live or die for?

Still other boys spend all their time talking about girls. I'm still young and other than Mom and our sister Zeruiah (I Chronicles 2:15-16), I really don't know much about girls. But these boys talk like there is nothing else in the world worth living for. I know God's first command to Adam was "be fruitful and multiply" and that one of the greatest drives that every male of every species has is to obey that command, but is that all there is to life? Is that a cause to die for?

Some boys from town spend all their time buying, selling, or trading sheep, cows, or other livestock. They try to make money doing this. They call it the "Livestock Market" or something like that. It doesn't seem to matter how much money they have. It is never enough. They always want more. Is making money a cause to live and die for?

When I heard Goliath curse the God of Israel, I felt like defending God and our homeland was a cause worth dying for. After all, we are the people entrusted with keeping God's Word for the world (Romans 3:2).

I know Goliath was huge (he is a half cubit shorter now since I took off his head), but is peace and safety to be traded for slavery to a pagan group of Philistines?

So I ask you again, dear brother, for which cause should I live? I love you, brother, and look forward to your answer.

Sincerely,
David

THE POTTER'S VASE
February 3, 2007

Dear Potter,

Now that it is over, I can see what you were making out of me and it all makes sense. I am thrilled and humbled at the same time to see that I am allowed to hold water and flowers for you on this amazing banquet table. To be able to be this close to the Creator of the universe is beyond my wildest dreams.

I am sorry that I complained so much all along the way as you worked on me. When you first took me out of the horrible pit (Psalm 40:2) and set me on solid ground, I was so happy. It was so great to see the light of day for the first time in my life!

It hurt me badly though when you began crushing me with your feet to look for lumps in me. (Isaiah 41:25) But now that you are finished, I understand why you could not allow rocks or dirt or any other impurities in me. I see now that as you molded me and shaped me on the spinning wheel, the impurities would have destroyed my shape—right in your hands (Jeremiah 18:4).

I know you could have made me into something else like a flowerpot or a toilet bowl since they are thicker and small impurities can be tolerated. But now, I am thankful you continued picking out flaws, in spite of the fact that it hurt me at that time.

When you had me all shaped and then set me on the shelf to dry, I was so despondent. I thought you were displeased with me—or had changed your mind about using me at all. As I sat there on the shelf for days, I wept day and night. There is probably still a wet spot where you had left me. Now I see that drying out is an essential step in this process. I'm sorry that I complained.

The worst part for me was the oven. It was so hot in there, that I felt myself getting a tough skin at first. And then, I was hardened through and through. I thought the oven time would never end. It was sad to see that so many others in there had cracked to pieces under the pressure and heat. I had known some of them since we were in the pit together.

Now that it is over, I see why the oven time was needed. Without it, I would be useless for the job for which you created me. The paint job you did on me is incredible! The glaze coating on me makes me look like I'm… well… fit for a King's table. Thanks for working with me. It is an honor to be with you.

Signed,
The Vase

STILL WAITING ON GOD
February 3, 2007

(the Motion for Reconsideration of our Motion for Acquittal is still on Judge Rodgers' desk. I know that many are praying for my release. This letter is based on Acts 12:5)

Dear Peter,

I have been following your case with great interest. I know that Herod has killed James and has had you arrested, tried, convicted, and sentenced to die in the morning (Acts 12:4). The situation looks impossible, Peter. You are bound with two chains between two Roman soldiers who are highly trained in the art of war. There are fourteen more stationed at the prison door to prevent a rescue or an escape. All of the soldiers know that if you escape, Roman law requires that they die. From a human perspective your case is hopeless.

I am watching you sleep, Peter. Thanks for trusting Me. More people are praying for you than you can imagine. I heard all their prayers, Peter. Situations like yours are where I do my best work. Watch this.

"Okay, Gabriel! Wake him up. You know what to do."

**Signed,
God**

WRITTEN FROM GOD TO MRS. JOB
February 3, 2007

Dear Mrs. Job,

I heard your prayers and I see your broken heart. I know that you grieve for all you have lost—your loving children, your wealth, and your security. I also know that your heart is broken as you see your husband suffer day after day outside the city. I know that you think he would be better off dead. I understand exactly how you feel. I also know that you are wondering if it will ever end. It will.

There is another side to this story, Mrs. Job, that you haven't seen. I have everything under control. You see, there is a little problem up here in heaven with a former employee that needs to be disciplined. You and your husband were hand-picked by me to be part of my plan because I knew you would both be faithful. I will explain it all to you someday. But for now....thanks for being faithful.

Signed,
God

PS *I suggest you start gathering diapers and other baby things again.*

WRITTEN FROM MORDECAI TO GOD
February 5, 2007
(based on Esther 3-4)

Dear God,

This is your servant Mordecai. I'm nervous about tomorrow. I need to unload on You a little bit. As You know, Haman the Agagite is planning to have all us Jews killed soon, and my cousin Esther is risking her life to go UNINVITED before the King in the morning. There is a great chance she will be killed (Esther 4:11).

God, as I think about this situation I can see many times where You could have stopped all this. Since You didn't, I'm nervous that You will also let all of us be killed. You could have had Saul or one of his soldiers kill Agag and his seed five hundred years ago (I Samuel 15:9). Why did You let one survive? You could have had King Ahasuerus promote someone else besides Haman (Esther 3:1). Why did You allow this man who hates your people to become so rich and powerful?

You could have stopped the law, allowing us to be killed, from passing. Why didn't You have the King or one of his counselors see the danger in this law?

If You are going to allow us to be killed, why did You allow the lot Haman cast to make the date eleven months away (Esther 3:13)? All your people will live in terror for nearly a year! Is that wise, God?

Lord, the law is passed. Your people are condemned to die. The date is set and the messengers have been sent out (Esther 3:13). The case is sealed, Lord. It looks hopeless! Now my precious cousin is planning to risk her life and approach the King without being invited. Lord, are You watching us suffer down here? Please God, do something!

Your Concerned Servant,
Mordecai

(Esther did go before the King and save her people. God often waits until the situation is looking hopeless so that only He can get the glory.)

LETTER FROM JESUS TO MARTHA
February 6, 2007
(based on Luke 10:38-42)

Dear Martha,

Thank you so much for allowing all of us to come to your home for a visit yesterday. I know that few people would welcome seventy people to their home on such short notice like that. You, Mary and Lazarus have always been such great friends and supporters of the work of God. The disciples had all been out preaching and needed a time of relaxation and refreshment. Thank you for providing for them.

As I'm sure you noticed yesterday, there is one area of concern I would like to share with you. You and Mary both love Me and would do anything for Me. There has never been a question about that. You show your devotion in different ways. You keep busy doing things, while Mary is more concerned about listening and learning.

Yesterday I told you that only one thing is needful and Mary had chosen it. Please consider that Adam and Eve had everything provided for them. All I wanted was their fellowship.

I want you to talk with Me more than you work for Me. In all of human history, there has been a strong tendency for people to try to rest in their work for Me, rather than to rest in Me. Their work becomes their security instead of Me. Their work for Me becomes an idol. I am a jealous God and don't share my glory with another (Deuteronomy 5:9). Isaiah 42:8 says, "I am the LORD: that is my name: and my glory will I not give to another, neither my praise to graven images."

So Martha, Martha, read my Word, talk with Me, and more importantly, come sit and listen to Me. I can take care of the food. Remember the loaves and fishes?

Love,
Jesus

THE MISSION FIELD IN G2O
March 4, 2007

(G2O means Escambia County Jail, Pensacola, Florida; Green Tower, Second floor, Orange door. Matthew 19:20 "And he said unto them, Go ye into all the world, and preach the gospel to every creature.")

Here is an update on my status. I am still in the Escambia County Jail—just over four months now. Our attorneys are still filing motions with District Judge Casey Rodgers to drop the charges, acquit the case, and release me from jail. When all of these are ruled on, if she does not overturn the case, it will go to the 11th Circuit Court of Appeals. The attorneys are still confident that we have broken no laws and will prevail. I am still not free to explain our side, but you can get many details on www.penaltyprotestor.com. Praise God! My wife's sentencing has been postponed indefinitely. We covet your prayers for my release as in Acts 12:5 and James 5:16.

The CSE Ministry Team is still doing well, in spite of the devastating blow. My son Eric has done an awesome job filling in for me during my "extended leave!" We still get dozens of reports every week of souls being saved and lives being changed. That is our main purpose on earth. We praise God for using us even during this great time of trial and testing.

In response to an overzealous newspaper article, Mark Twain once wrote, "The reports of my recent death are greatly exaggerated." Likewise, Dinosaur Adventure Land still has visitors from all over the globe, in spite of many false reports about it being closed.

The "church" at G2O is doing well also. Our three times per day Bible Study and Prayer Times are a great joy! The Holy Spirit is changing lives in unbelievable ways. The jail offers a six week class to help those with addictions. It is taught once a week in this particular jail pod. Therefore, men who request this class are placed in this pod in order to most efficiently teach the class. This keeps a continued flow of men to my pod, yet God has kept me in the same place. I guess you could say the Church in G2O is very transient!

If you have never read the book, "Peace Child" by missionary Don Richardson, you should! It is available from the CSE web-site. I re-read the book every few years to renew my evangelistic zeal. In the book, missionary Don went to reach the head-hunting, cannibalistic Sawi Tribe in the swamps of Papua New Guinea.

He soon discovered that he had to learn not only a new language and culture, but a totally new way of thinking. In the Sawi culture, treachery using the basest deceit was the highest virtue!! As Don shared the gospel story with the Sawis, they came to the conclusion that Judas Iscariot was the hero! Based on their worldview, this was a logical conclusion. Read this amazing book to learn how he overcame this great obstacle.

My last four months in jail have been similar in many ways. Most of the men God sent me to reach in here have a very different way of viewing the world and thinking about many things. In one Bible study, I mentioned that God's plan is for both the man and the woman to be virgins on their wedding day and to stay faithful for life. I said that is what my wife and I have done for over thirty three years. No one in this jail pod had ever heard of such a thing! One man said, "That would be so cool! You could really trust your wife and have a great relationship, couldn't you!"

Just as Don had to spend hours listening to the Sawis to understand their culture before he found the key to reaching them for Christ; I have spent untold hours listening to men who were raised completely opposite of me, describe their world view. It is important to "sit where they sit" to really reach them (Ezekiel 3:15). Understanding the reasons behind why they take drugs, wear pants halfway down with their boxers showing, have gold front teeth, have 16" long dread locks that they have not combed in eight years, or flock to the TV for the local news to see if their "home-boy" was arrested, is all part of my current missionary assignment.

I have seen men shake and sweat as they come off some of the worst drugs known to man. I learned that black men can shave with a plastic spoon! I see the results of the failure of our society, school system, and churches. Why weren't these men reached when they were kids?

I've been able to witness to Muslims, Buddhists, Nazis, drug dealers, Jehovah Witnesses, whoremongers, adulterers, child molesters, and homosexuals, as well as men who have no clue who their father is and whose mother was a prostitute. Most have never been to church or read the Bible in their entire life.

Watching them get excited about learning God's Word after they trust Christ is a sight of which I never tire! God wakes me up about 3:30 every morning so I walk to each man's "house" and pray for them by name. The fact that many have probably never had anyone pray for them breaks my heart every day. What a mission field!

Thank you for continuing to pray for me and the CSE Team. Keep spreading the gospel!

For Souls,
Kent Hovind

ANOTHER NEW MISSION FIELD PART 1
March 8, 2007

(based on Mark 16:15 "And he said unto them, Go ye into all the world, and preach the gospel to every creature.")

4:00 am Awoke to lights on

4:30 am Given breakfast

5:00 am Heard PA announcement, "Bunk Three, Hovind, H O V I N D, ATW" (ATW means you are going home!)

5:00 - 5:30 am Packed up stuff and gave books away to inmates

5:30 am Had prayer time with ten men who love Jesus and me, to ask God's blessing as I leave to go home

5:45 am Heard PA announcement, "Correction to earlier announcement. Bunk Three, Hovind, H O V I N D, no ATW—being transported."

5:46 am Taken by guards down to sit in the ice cold "tank" and wait

6:30 am Moved by car to a different part of the jail to another freezing cold "tank" to wait

9:10 am Saw Federal Marshals arrive to transport me to a Federal Prison Camp in Pensacola. This minimum security federal facility was designed for 300 but houses 700 men. All these men work to help maintain military bases in the area.

11:00 am Finish intake details including a physical. Lost 25 pounds in the County Jail

11:15 am Served first good hot food in four and a half months!

12:00-10:00 pm Free to roam, well, sort of free. For the first time in four and a half months, I felt a blade of grass; wore tie shoes, a belt, and a real shirt and pants (no jump suit!); got a locker with a lock; and slept on a bed with a real pillow. Feeling the sunshine for only the fourth time in four and a half months made me want to walk around the camp all day!

ANOTHER NEW MISSION FIELD PART 2
March 9, 2007

11:30-2:00 pm Scrubbed pots and pans

2:00-5:00 pm Scrubbed down a grill as health inspection is coming up. My boss loved my work! He said it is the best the grill has looked in years.

There is a video library here, and our creation video tapes have been here for many years. They were very well worn. They were also removed the afternoon after I arrived. There seem to be many men who had watched them and know me and who have followed my case during the past months. Several concerned brothers showed me around and supplied me with things I needed, including a watch and tennis shoes. God is sooooo good!

I will get full-contact visits beginning Friday evening, Saturday, and Sunday! My family only lives six and one half miles away! The vast majority of the men here are far away from their families. It has been so hard not to be able to touch my family or hold my grandchildren. I have never held my newest grandson, Eric Jordan.

There are no bars or locked gates and no sickening sounds of steel doors slamming shut. There are private showers and toilets, vending machines, and coke and ice! I will never look at many simple things in life the same.

There are twelve men in my small room. At least five are professing Christians, two are Jews, and I don't know about the rest yet. I started a Bible study with one guy, but before we finished, twelve more joined. There are only 688 more men to go! It's a little overwhelming at first. What a mission field! I have learned, however, that group meetings/Bible studies must be limited to no more than five in a group at a time. This rule was a direct result of 9/11. It will take more patience and time to reach men this way, but God knows all these things.

The Motion for Acquittal of Counts 13 - 57 is still on Judge Rodger's desk. If she grants that, she will have to re-sentence me. Then the 11th Circuit will get our Motion for Release Pending Appeal.

Thanks for your faithful prayers. I will never forget the great time with God in the county jail. Truly, His grace is sufficient! Many men's lives were changed for this life and for eternity. They still love to get mail and tracts. My new, hopefully short-term, address is:

Kent Hovind #06452-017
110 Raby Avenue
Pensacola, FL 32509

Thank you for continuing to pray for me and the CSE Team.
Keep spreading the gospel!
Acts 12:5

CHURCH IN G2O
April 18, 2007

(based on 3 John 4 "I have no greater joy than to hear that my children walk in the truth.")

During my four-month stay in the Escambia County Jail, I had the joy of seeing 17 men accept Christ as Savior. Most grew rapidly in the Lord as they attended our three Bible studies a day. Now that I have been gone for over a month, the two men I left in charge sent our office the following report. The names have been left out and the bunk numbers have been changed, but each represents a real man—either one who is growing in the Lord, or one who needs Him. The asterisks represent men who trusted Christ while I "pastored the Church in G2O." Praise God!

Dear Mr. Kent,

God bless you and everything you have done. All of us are praying for you to be released, and I believe that you will be sooner than you think. The seed that Jesus brought you here to plant has taken deep root. We have had many new additions, and thanks be to God, we were able to help a man pray to ask Jesus to be his Savior! Here's an update on G2O.

Bunk #1 - A lost soul without a care for anyone but himself.

Bunk #2 - A new and consistently active member of Bible study. Grew up an Awana member earning the II Timothy 2:15 award as a child. Strayed from God but through the Bible study is back and living for God's will.

Bunk #3 - A hardcore street thug who knows nothing but guns, drugs, and violence. He was someone Dave and I never thought would attend Bible study! Never in a million years! But one night out of the blue he came with a conscience of terrible guilt to bare. He has come to every Bible Study since. I have never seen an answer to prayer like this! A true miracle from Bunk #3!

Bunk #4 - A lost soul.

Bunk #5 - When Eric and Jo came to visit us, they said you were still praying for several men in G2O. We relayed this message to Bunk #5 and he came to Bible study that night. He is still caught up in the "hood lifestyle" but he has a conscience. One day, he will turn to God! Keep praying!

Bunk #6 - Comes to every single Bible study! Reads the Bible you sent him day and night! Takes his convictions seriously. He has totally changed since he came to G2O. He is a new man!

Bunk #7 - Lost soul. No progress with him yet.

Bunk #8 - Now leads the Bible Study and is fervent in his heart about what God has planned for him. Has been blessed beyond his wildest dreams.

Bunk #9 - Was coming to every Bible Study and was reading the Bible you sent him pretty regularly, but the State came at him with a twenty-year sentence. Now instead of coming to Bible Study, he's cussing, playing cards and worse things that I don't want to mention. If he doesn't change soon, I fear he will indeed get the 20 year sentence and worse from God.

Bunk #10 - You, as I'm sure you remember, had your ministry provide him a Defenders Study Bible. He came a few times to Bible Study after you left, then stopped. He was just sentenced to ten years federal prison time and eight years probation afterward; and will be transferred within two weeks. We still love him and will keep praying for him.

Bunk #11 - Comes to almost every Bible study, but needs to work on his actions. Still cusses and gambles. But he has a conscience and knows he's wrong for it.

Bunk #12 - Attends Bible study regularly and had one of his charges dropped—what a blessing. Still cusses and needs work on attitude.

Bunk #13 - Newcomer that just started attending Bible study.

Bunk #14 - New comer whose Dad was a preacher. Attends Bible study, but thinks he knows a better way. Obviously, his way didn't work for him. We think he still needs Jesus.

Bunk #15 - Attends every Bible study. Loves the new Bible you had gotten him only two days before you left G2O.

Bunk #16 - Comes to every Bible study. Just had his V.O.P. dropped and his five-year sentence reduced to 18 months and rehab! Needs a Bible.

Bunk #17 - Totally lost!

Bunk #18 - Me...working hard to do God's will. I keep falling short, but I'm learning. Co-leader of the Bible study.

Bunk #19 - Accepted Jesus Christ only two days after coming to G2O!

Bunk #20 - Attends every Bible study. Loves God in all HIS glory.

Bunk #21 - Still lost even after crying on his knees with another man. He just won't let go and let God! He thinks he can save himself!

Bunk #22 - Troublemaker. Satan himself! Pray that he will be moved as he does nothing but try to disrupt the Bible studies!

God bless you, Mr. Kent. We are praying non-stop for God to get you released, but we will be forever grateful for the "Church in G2O" founded by you, Mr. Kent. God be with you!"

WHY SUFFERING?
April 22, 2007

(based on James 5:10 Take, my brethren, the prophets, who have spoken in the name of the Lord, for an example of suffering affliction, and of patience.")

When things happen that we consider to be bad, or that causes suffering, it is normal to ask why. Everyone I know has had bad things happen to them. Some of these things are permanently life-altering like my 21-year-old niece who broke her back last year and is now confined to a wheelchair or my son-in-law Paul whose life was taken with cancer at such a young age. Some are long term like my prison sentence. Some trials are of unknown duration. People have no idea when, if ever, the suffering will end. Some suffering, like being sentenced to hell, will be eternal. Why does God allow His creatures to suffer?

The question of why God allows suffering has been asked since man was expelled from the Garden of Eden. When my wife and I were convicted and I was sentenced, yes, it caused us to ask the "why" question again.

Many books have been written and thousands of sermons preached on this topic. I won't add anything new I'm sure. I won't pretend to know the why in my situation, but here are my thoughts.

Some suffering is simply part of being human. Jesus was tired (Matthew 8:24), hungry (Matthew 4:2), thirsty (John 19:28) and even died yet had no sin.

1. *Some suffering is allowed by God as a purifying grace (Job 23:19, Hebrews 12:1-12).*
2. *Some is a result of our disobedience or sin (I Peter 4:15).*
3. *Some, like military boot camp, is to prepare us for greater service in God's kingdom now or later when He sets up His kingdom on earth (Matthew 25:21).*
4. *God may allow some to suffer in order to help others (II Corinthians 1:4).*
5. *God may allow some to suffer to "show them off" to Satan (Job).*

So why did this happen to Kent Hovind?

God may have sent me to prison:

1. *To reach people here that need the gospel (Acts 8:26, Phillipians 4:22).*
2. *To be salt and light (Matthew 5:13-14).*
3. *To prepare me for greater future use in the creation science ministry.*
4. *To help prepare someone else for future use (Genesis 50:20).*
5. *To give me a taste of the coming New World Order to enhance my preaching.*
6. *To help motivate others to Christian service.*
7. *To better understand the multitude of people in jail. Since over two million Americans are currently incarcerated (the highest per capita in the world!) God may have wanted to open my eyes to the great injustices being done and to let me, like Ezekiel, see the plight of these people in order that I might more effectively minister to them.*
8. *To be an advocate of returning to more Biblical forms of punishment. When the judge ordered punishment in the Bible, the judge himself had to witness the punishment. Few judges today ever actually see the consequences of the sentences that they hand down to the offender and his family. Maybe all judges should be required to visit both the ones that they incarcerate and his family several times each year?*
9. *To understand the trial of faith that comes from taking a stand for righteous issues as Daniel did concerning eating meats.*
10. *To understand the consequences of taking a stand on issues that were right, but could cause a weaker brother to stumble.*

Above all, God is still in charge. I willingly submit to this chapter of my life in order that I may become a more profitable servant for HIS glory.

Kent

LETTER FROM GOD TO PRINCE MALCHIAH?
May 4, 2007
(written from the hole aka solitary confinement – based on Jeremiah 38:5-13)

Dear Prince Malchiah,

I'm angry with you! You allowed those evil friends of yours to use your well to torture my prophet Jeremiah. It was you that volunteered the use of it! Have you ever been treated this way? How would you feel if you were waist deep in mud, starving, cold, and terrified at the bottom of a well?

As a prince, you will be held to a higher standard. I allowed you to have authority and power over others' lives and you abused it (Luke 11:46). Did you enjoy that feeling of absolute power as you looked down on your helpless victim? Did you ever stop to think that what you sow, you will reap (Galatians 6:7)?

Why does power and authority corrupt people like you? Why don't you thank me for promoting you and bless all those under your authority?

Jeremiah only repeated what I told him to say and you hurt him badly. He is my prophet. When the king of Babylon takes this city, you will die and face me over this issue and many more. Get ready for our appointment (Amos 4:12)!

God

LETTER FROM GOD TO POTIPHAR?
May 4, 2007
(written from the hole aka solitary confinement – based on Genesis 39)

Dear Potiphar,

I entrusted Joseph, one of My most precious children to your care. You took good care of him for years. He was faithful and worked hard for you. Then, last week, your wife lied about him and you believed her. You have known her for a long time and know not to trust her. You have also known Joseph for a long time and know you can trust him.

Now Joseph is chained in prison. His legs are bleeding from the shackles.

> *Psa 105: ^{17} He sent a man before them, even Joseph, who was sold for a servant: ^{18} Whose feet they hurt with fetters: he was laid in iron:*

Potiphar, I'm angry at what you have done. I'll judge you later about this. You have never been chained up in a cage Potiphar. You have no idea what your five-second decision made in a rage is doing to one of my children. He will suffer for years while you enjoy life.

But we have an appointment, Potiphar. One day you will die; and then we will talk about this (Hebrew 9:27).

Talk to you later,
God

LETTER FROM NOAH TO GOD?
May 4, 2007
(written from the hole aka solitary confinement – based on Genesis 7:10)

Dear God,

I've been sitting in this ark for five days now! Nothing has happened Lord. I have spent my entire life savings on this giant boat in the middle of a field just like you told me to do, Lord. People have laughed at me and my family for many years now. We tried to ignore them and kept building, but their insults hurt.

We all trusted you to guide us. All eight of us sold everything and moved into the boat just like you instructed. We have a lot of animals in here, Lord, and it is starting to smell. The people outside are still laughing at us, Lord! It has been five days since You shut the door. Lord, are you listening? Did we do all this for nothing?

I love you, Lord, and I trust you; but sometimes I just don't understand why You wait. I did everything you said, and now I look like a fool to my neighbors! God! Are you listening?

I've got to go feed the animals now, Lord, but I still would like an answer. We'll talk more later.

Noah

LETTER FROM THE AX TO THE WOODSMAN
May 15, 2007
(written from Tallahassee Prison – based on 2 Samuel 22:31 "As for God, his way is perfect; the word of the LORD is tried: he is a buckler to all them that trust in him.")

Dear Woodsman,

Why have you done this? We were doing so well felling trees for the Master's house and you quit chopping with me in the middle of cutting that big oak. Why? I was doing my best. I never flew off the handle. I cut as deep as I could every swing. What did I do wrong?

Why do you have me clamped in this vice? I can't move! I can't chop wood here. I was designed for chopping wood. I love it! Please don't leave me clamped in this vice. I feel pressure on my sides that I've never felt before. I can handle the pressure on my cutting edge. Go ahead. Chop with me all day long. I can take it. Actually, I love it!

Now what? No! Wait! Why are you grinding and filing off part of me? Why would you take away pieces of the most effective part of me—my cutting edge?

Woodsman, the Master needs the trees cut! This delay is holding up the job we were doing for Him! Please stop grinding on me and get me out of this vice. I want to go back to work. I love cutting wood. Ouch! You are hurting me!

Woodsman, are you listening to me? Do you know what you are doing?
The Ax

LETTER FROM THE WOODSMAN TO THE AX
May 24, 2007

(written by a Blog Contributor – I don't know who this blog contributor is, but their blog blessed me to tears as I sat in the South Carolina prison! This is the only letter not written by the author, but it fits the theme so well, that I had to include it.)

Dear Ax,

Do you not trust the hands of your woodsman who has swung you all this time? I have never dropped you. Never laid you idle. Never swung you wrong. Never let you rust... Never forgotten you.

My dear Ax, bold and strong, you have done nothing wrong. Trust your woodsman. I know you can't feel the strong grip of my hands you know so well. Try not to struggle. Ax... Ax... focus on me, on the sound of my voice. Ax... Ax... do not look away; focus on my face. Don't turn away from me. I know it is difficult to understand this. I know you are in pain.

And yes, the oak... we have worked together clearing many forests... dead and decaying rot and timber. You have done well and continue to hold up under the great building pressure. I know it hurts. I know your pain. An answer will come in time. Pain, though it hurts, does not mean something bad is happening. You will understand in time why I grind your best places off of you. You are doing well.

I do hear you, Ax. Do you hear me? I do know what I am doing. The Master expects the best of us and the Master knows of my doings. The trees will be there. Trust the hands of your woodsman.

The Woodsman

LETTER FROM GOD TO URBANE
May 19, 2007

(written during my eight-day stay at the United States Penitentiary Maximum Security Holding Unit in Atlanta—one of the worst prisons in the system. Based on Romans 16:9 "Salute Urbane, our helper in Christ, and Stachys my beloved.")

Dear Urbane,

I just thought I'd write you a quick note to let you know I saw all the things you did to help my servant Paul. I know there seems to be more glory in being the preacher like Paul, but your help in setting up chairs and sweeping the floor and helping people park their camels is important too!

Those great revivals wouldn't run smoothly without you and others like you. I know you don't do it to get glory or be famous, but Urbane, I see your heart and I like what I see.

I'm going to make you famous anyway. Hundreds of millions of people are going to read about you, son. Your name will be listed in My Word which will be the world's all-time best selling book!

Keep up the good work and keep your servant's heart. I've got a place prepared for you that you won't believe! I'll see you there in a few years!

**Love,
God**

LETTER FROM PETER TO GOD
May 19, 2007

(written during my eight-day stay at the United States Penitentiary Maximum Security Holding Unit in Atlanta—one of the worst prisons in the system. Based on Acts 12:4-4 "Now about that time Herod the king stretched forth his hands to vex certain of the church. And he killed James the brother of John with the sword. And because he saw it pleased the Jews, he proceeded further to take Peter also. (Then were the days of unleavened bread.) And when he had apprehended him, he put him in prison, and delivered him to four quaternions of soldiers to keep him; intending after Easter to bring him forth to the people.")

Dear God,

We have a serious situation here Lord! I need You to listen closely. Do you remember my best friend, James; you know, as in "Peter, James, and John—the inner circle?" Well, he is dead, Lord. Herod killed him yesterday. Today Herod arrested me.

Now Lord, all we have done for years is try to serve you. We left our nets and followed You for three and a half years. "And they straightway left their nets, and followed him"(Matthew 4:20). Since then, we have been preaching and teaching just like You told us to do. We are trying to do Your will, God. But now James is dead, and I'm in jail. God, are you watching us down here?

Lord, I'm cold sitting on this rock floor. My feet and hands hurt from the cold, heavy, sharp chains. I can't even roll over, Lord. I've got a big Roman soldier on each side of me. These guys are heartless, Lord. They seem to enjoy making prisoners miserable.

I just want you to know what's happening, Lord. I'm real uncomfortable, a little nervous, and scheduled to die soon. I'm willing to go back out preaching, Lord; but You will have to work a miracle fast.

Don't forget about me, okay? Are you listening? I trust you, Lord; so I'm going to sleep.

Love,
Peter

LETTER FROM GOD TO EBED-MELECH
May 20, 2007

(written during my eight-day stay at the United States Penitentiary Maximum Security Holding Unit in Atlanta—one of the worst prisons in the system. Based on Jeremiah 38:7-13 " Now when Ebed-melech the Ethiopian, one of the eunuchs which was in the king's house, heard that they had put Jeremiah in the dungeon; the king then sitting in the gate of Benjamin; Ebed-melech went forth out of the king's house, and spake to the king, saying, My lord the king, these men have done evil in all that they have done to Jeremiah the prophet, whom they have cast into the dungeon; and he is like to die for hunger in the place where he is: for there is no more bread in the city. Then the king commanded Ebed-melech the Ethiopian, saying, Take from hence thirty men with thee, and take up Jeremiah the prophet out of the dungeon, before he die. So Ebed-melech took the men with him, and went into the house of the king under the treasury, and took thence old cast clouts and old rotten rags, and let them down by cords into the dungeon to Jeremiah. And Ebed-melech the Ethiopian said unto Jeremiah, Put now these old cast clouts and rotten rags under thine armholes under the cords. And Jeremiah did so. So they drew up Jeremiah with cords, and took him up out of the dungeon: and Jeremiah remained in the court of the prison.")

Dear Ebed-melech,

Thank you for what you did for my preacher, Jeremiah. I saw the whole thing, son. You did great! I know your life has not been the best. I saw when you were sold into slavery and taken from your family. I saw when you were made a eunuch and your dreams of marriage and family were destroyed. I know some people here look down on you just because you are black. I know you have many good reasons to hate life. Thank you for not being bitter!

I also know that my preacher Jeremiah is not very popular right now. I know Nebuchadnezzar is camped around the city. I sent him (Jeremiah

38:3). I know the people hate Jeremiah for his preaching about surrender, but that's what I told him to preach.

I saw when Pashur and his evil men threw my preacher into the dungeon full of mire. I heard them laugh at him struggling in the filth. I knew their very thoughts.

I also saw your compassion on him, Ebed. I know you are all so weak, it took thirty of you to pull him out. Thanks for thinking of the old rags for padding so that the rope wouldn't hurt him. That was very kind.

Ebed, this city is going to be destroyed, but you will be spared (Jeremiah 39:16-18). I'm also preparing a home for you up here with Me that is more than you could dream about in a million years.

Keep up the good work, son, and keep watching out for ways to help My preachers. They need guys like you.

Love,
God

THE ORDER OF THE ARROW
May 20, 2007

I loved Boy Scouts! It was a great experience for me in many ways. I became Eagle Scout in 1968 at age fifteen. I still have fond memories of working hard for sometimes hundreds of hours to get a pin, a medal, or a patch. It felt so good to complete the task! I still have my coat, completely covered in patches in my closet.

Once you have earned an award, it gives you a feeling of accomplishment, which is sweet (Proverbs 13:19), but it also gives you a feeling of comradery with others who have earned the same award.

I would spend hours at the scout rifle range trying to get a perfect score of fifty—ten bulls-eyes in a row! As I earned various pins for marksmanship, I would begin to notice other boys wearing the same pin. Almost like magic, we were drawn to each other to talk and become friends. Without a word being spoken about it, we each knew the hours of patience and practice and discipline the other had endured. It made us "brothers."

I remember one year when I earned the Order of the Arrow! To get this award, you had to be isolated for 24 hours in the woods without food and you could not say one word. That was almost forty years ago, and I don't recall all the details of it, but that was the general idea. If you made it through this ordeal, you, brave warrior, could wear the arrow sash! This put you in a class just under God with the other scouts! You were a man now!

Over the years, I've earned various awards like three chess tournament trophies in high school and letters for tennis, but the past twelve months, July 2006 through July 2007, I've earned many that will make me "brothers" with millions of people both dead and alive. You would have to be there to understand.

I have been through the ordeal of public arrest; court; jail; front-page news; diesel therapy; solitary confinement; lousy food and beds; cold showers; loud, obnoxious swearing cell mates; snoring cell mates; uncertainty; "the hole;" "the tank;" ugly jump suits; freezing cells; some arrogant, power-hungry guards without compassion; stand-up counts; claustrophobia in seven-by-twelve-foot cells locked in twenty-three hours per day; hunger; tears by the bucket; long lonely days and nights; blaring televisions broadcasting dumb shows announcing "You are not the father!"; "recreation" with an egg-shaped, slick basketball in a chain link cage; "inspections" where guards just take whatever they want; recorded phone calls; "visits" through a glass on a phone that is forty-years-old; and breakfast that is the same bland stuff every day at 4:30 a.m.

I have seen guys fight over dumb stuff, worn "the jewelry" of handcuffs and leg shackles, taken five-hour bus rides in chairs and shaved with the cheapest razor on earth. I've seen guys get tattooed with burned paper mixed with deodorant and pushed under the skin with a staple sharpened on the dirty concrete. I've seen many get staph infections that way.

I've seen the look on men's faces when the judge gives them twenty years, or their wife writes for a divorce. I've sat and cried and prayed with grown men whose lives were coming unglued. I've seen men light smuggled cigarettes with a battery and a razor blade. I've heard how drugs have destroyed men's lives as well as their family. I've seen the men with rotten teeth from dope.

I've had to kneel on the floor and back up to the little hole in the door to be handcuffed behind my back to move ten feet to take a shower. I've sat on the freezing toilets with no privacy.

I've seen the warden take a good man's furlough away the night before for no reason other than because he felt like it. Even though plane tickets had been purchased and plans had been made for six months and it was for the nine-year-old daughter's birthday, who hadn't hugged her dad in six years!

I've been in rooms where an idiot painted latex paint over oil-base paint and watched as it pealed off in big sheets. I've been searched and strip searched, "breath-a-lyzed" and drug tested. I've slept on old lumpy two inch thick mattresses with no pillow in rooms of concrete and steel that echo with every whisper.

I've seen guys heat water with a "stinger," make rope out of garbage bags, and pass notes between cells on a bar of soap. I've used a roll of toilet paper for a pillow. I've been crammed in a ten by twelve foot room with twenty men while the guards slowly did their job between telling hunting stories.

I've sharpened my pencils on the concrete floor and gone days with no paper or pencil because the CO (correctional officer) was too lazy to get one for me. I've seen "counselors" ignore inmates' urgent requests for attorney calls.

I've strained to understand the guard's unintelligible announcements over the scratchy PA system. I've swept the floor with a twenty year old broom that is two feet tall and has eleven straws left. I've brushed my teeth with the lousiest toothpaste on earth with a brush two-and-one-half inches long. I've been moved four times—always the day before commissary—and I arrive the day after commissary at the new location. I've seen scores of men sleep on the floor due to the tremendous overcrowding. I've tried to shave looking in the "mirror" that is a badly scratched cookie sheet bolted to the wall. I've worn the pink underwear because some idiot in the laundry washed it with the orange jump suits.

I've been fingerprinted six times and filled out the very same form seven times. I've watched as inmates try to plaster vents shut with wet toilet paper to keep the freezing-cold air out. I've heard the sickening mechanical, heartless thud over 1,000 times, as the heavy steel door locks to seal you in. I've seen miles of razor wire on acres of chain link fences. I've been moved hundreds of miles from my family for no reason, by a system that doesn't care. I know full well the feeling of being hopelessly trapped in the belly of a great beast who really doesn't worry about anyone in it. I know the long days and nights of yearning to hold my family in my arms.

But, I have seen men come humbly to God and grow in ways that are miraculous. Yes, I've earned a few badges this year and now I'm brother to about thirty million other Americans, plus countless others worldwide throughout the centuries, who have the same badge! I will use it to win souls. The badge feels good—because God does give grace for the test!

Kent
I Corinthians 4
I Corinthians 9
II Corinthians 11

Why On Earth Did God Let This Happen... For Heaven's Sake?

LETTER FROM DANIEL TO GOD
May 20, 2007

(written during my eight-day stay at the United States Penitentiary Maximum Security Holding Unit in Atlanta—one of the worst prisons in the system. Based on Daniel Chapter 6)

Dear God,

I hate to complain, but, I'm sitting in a den of lions! Thanks for closing their mouths and keeping me safe. Lord, I've been tested all my life. I was a teen when my country was destroyed and my family slain. I had to watch it all. Then, they made me a eunuch and destroyed my hope of having my own family. To top it off, I was dragged all the way to Babylon and made to work for the very people who did all this to us!

I've been faithful, Lord. In spite of everything, I've always prayed and read my Scroll. I've been bold for You. I have even witnessed to the king (Daniel 5) in spite of the fact that he has total power and a violent temper.

I heard how you protected my three friends from the fiery furnace while I was away on business, and I watched you protect me when Babylon fell to the Medes and the Persians (Daniel 5:28-31). Even when those evil men passed that dumb law about prayer (Daniel 6), I was faithful to pray to You (Daniel 6:11).

And now, I'm sitting in a den of lions at age ninety-three. Does the testing ever stop, Lord? I am tired. Do I deserve a retirement yet? I love You, Lord, and I trust You, but I don't always understand You.

Thanks for the soft lion to lean on, Lord. At my age, that really helps. But Lord, I do have one last request before I go to sleep. Would you please make that frisky lion cub stop pulling off my socks? I'm too old and tired to play today.

Thanks!
Daniel

KNEE-MAIL BETWEEN GOD AND KENT ON A FEW QUESTIONS
May 23, 2007

KH: Do you have time for a few questions, today, Lord?

GOD: Son, time has no effect on me. I created it. I am always here to help you and guide you in any area of your life. Go ahead with your questions, son.

KH: These last seven months in prison have been rather difficult for me, Lord. In fact, in the last month, I've been in five different facilities.

GOD: I know, son. I've been with you the entire time (Hebrews 13:5).

KH: Thanks, Lord. I felt your presence many times. But there were other times that I was very sad and lonely.

GOD: I know, son. I saw your tears. I was there, but you were too busy acting like Jonah. You were more concerned about your own problems than the future of those men around you. You need to work on that.

KH: I'm sorry, Lord. You are right.

GOD: I am always right. Go ahead with your questions.

KH: Well God, yesterday was especially hard. I couldn't sleep the night before because I expected them to call me at 3:30 a.m. to pack up for the bus ride up here to South Carolina.

GOD: I know, son. I was right there with you. I heard your prayers throughout that long night. We had sweet fellowship, didn't we, son? Thank you for loving me and talking with me.

KH: Thanks for being there and for listening, Lord.

GOD: I'm always there and always listening, son.

KH: Lord, I asked you to let me sleep, because I knew the next day would be hard and I would need my strength. Why didn't you let me sleep, Lord?

GOD: I did, son. You slept great from 3:00 - 4:45 a.m. Who do you think it was that made the guard forget to call you at 3:30? Didn't you wake up refreshed at 4:45 and even comment on how hard you slept and how good you felt?

KH: Yes, Lord, now that you remind me, I did sleep real hard and woke up feeling great.

GOD: Did you have the strength to make it through the day, son?

KH: Yes, Lord. I did.

GOD: I will always supply your need each day, son (Philippians 4:19). Quit worrying.

KH: I see that, Lord. But Lord, I was dreading that long bus ride locked in a cage like an animal wearing leg shackles and being handcuffed to a chain around my waist. It's real uncomfortable, Lord.

GOD: Yes, son. I know all about being treated badly and being real uncomfortable. But, son, have other men gone through this before?

KH: Yes, Lord. Millions have.

GOD: Will you have more compassion for these men now, son?

KH: Oh, yes, Lord. I will.

GOD: How many men were on that bus, son?

KH: There were forty, Lord.

GOD: Whose name was called to be the orderly and pass out food and water?

KH: Mine was, Lord.

GOD: That got you out of wearing the chains for the entire trip, didn't it, son?

KH: Yes, Lord. It did.

GOD: Who do you think arranged that?

KH: You did, Lord.

GOD: That's right, son. I heard your prayer and answered it. Relax, son. I have everything under control.

KH: I'm sorry, Lord. I worry too much.

GOD: Yes you do, son. You need to work on that. Did you get to minister to those men and witness to Jerome on the bus?

KH: Yes, I did, Lord.

GOD: Did you know his mother was a prostitute and that he has no idea who his father is? Did you know no one had ever prayed for him or witnessed to him in his entire life (Psalms 142:4)?

KH: No, Lord, I didn't know that.

GOD: Did you know he has been seeking me for three weeks now and I arranged everything for you to sit by him on that bus?

KH: No, Lord. I had no idea.

GOD: Did you know that he will meditate on My Word which you sowed in his heart and will get saved in seventeen days. He will later witness to his family and friends and by the time you all get up here for judgement day, eighty-seven people will be here because of him.

KH: I had no idea, Lord.

GOD: You have no idea about a lot of things, son. Would a two-and-a-half-hour bus ride in a cage be a small price to pay for eighty-seven souls? For even one soul?

KH: Yes, Lord. A real small price.

GOD: Quit griping, son. I know what I'm doing.

KH: I'll work on that, Lord.

GOD: Son, when you were in Atlanta and they locked twenty-four of you in that 14' x 20' room for two hours waiting to be processed out, what did you hear?

KH: I heard constant swearing and using your name in vain, Lord. It was awful!

GOD: I heard it all, too, son. I was in there with you. I also saw how it grieved your soul (II Peter 2:7-8). That is good, son. Ezekiel was grieved when he saw the sin of Israel (Ezekiel 8). Did you see the Asian man watching you from across the cell?

KH: Yes, Lord, I did.

GOD: His name is Sing. I've been working on him, son. I have great plans for his life. You can help him grow. Did you witness to Leroy while you were in there?

KH: I tried, Lord, but it was so crowded and so loud. I don't know if any of it got through.

GOD: My Word never comes back void, son (Isaiah 55:1). It got through. He has been in prison for fourteen years and has five more to go. He is angry at the world and planned to seek vengeance when he got out. He has been talking to me since yesterday. You won't see him again on earth, son, but his new cell mate is a Christian. In the next thirty days, he will witness to him and he will call on me for forgiveness. You will see him in Heaven, son.

KH: I had no idea, Lord.

GOD: You have no idea about lots of things, son. Quit griping and trust Me. I don't make mistakes.

KH: I know, Lord. I'm sorry.

GOD: You also had time to talk to John, but you never did. You were too busy trying to rest and asking me to have your appeal granted. I will overturn your case, son, when I'm done using you for this special mission. Do you think the US government or the Bureau of Prisons could hold you if I wanted you out?

KH: No, Lord. But you opened the prison for Peter in Acts 5:19 and 12:7, and for Joseph (Genesis 41), and even the grave for some people (John 11). I was just wondering if you loved them more than me or something, or maybe I had some sin you were punishing me for.

GOD: I love you more than your little brain could ever comprehend. You do have plenty of sin—though that's not why you are there. We will keep working on that sin list regardless of where you are.

KH: Thanks, Lord. Please do keep working on me.

GOD: Oh, I will, son. I'll finish the work which I started in you (Philippians 1:6). While I'm working on you, I will also work through you. Haven't you asked me to do that?

KH: Yes, Lord, many times.

GOD: You have asked me to use you 173,216 times in the past thirty-eight years, son. I am using you and will continue. Are you wanting to restrict when and where I can do that?

KH: Well...uhh...no, Lord. When I said send me anywhere, I guess I wasn't thinking about prison. We have given thousands of tapes and books to prisons and I've preached in dozens of them, Lord. I have traveled many miles preaching for the past seventeen years. Based on the calls and letters we have received, lots of souls have trusted You and many lives have been changed as a result. I was trying to obey You, Lord. I still want to serve You, but just not in here.

GOD: You are doing fine, son. You are still in my will. I've got you right where I want you. Do you remember how I called Philip to leave that great revival in Samaria to go to the desert and win that one black eunuch to me (Acts 8:26)?

KH: Yes, Lord.

GOD: He left his family for a while too, son. The revival continued in Samaria without him, and your ministry will continue without you for a while. Your son is doing a fine job and that staff I sent to work with you is totally dedicated to me, son. Everything will be fine. The videos and books will win souls for many years yet. Relax. By the way, son, that one black man that Philip reached that day in the desert spread my gospel to his entire country of Ethiopia and later, all of Africa was opened to the gospel. Philip wondered why I pulled him out of his busy, successful ministry to go reach just one soul. Now that he's been here for two thousand years and has seen the fruit still coming in from his effort in the desert, he understands real well. Philip is watching you (Hebrews 12:1). He's cheering you on. He says, "Hi." His mansion is near yours. You two have a lot in common, son. His family worked in his ministry as well (Acts 21:8-9). You and he will have plenty of time to talk when you get up here.

KH: Lord, tell him I said, "Hi, and thanks for cheering."

GOD: When you get out, son, you will be a lot better equipped to reach even more people than before. Now you understand what thirty million other Americans have been through, plus many millions more in other countries. By the way, son, how did you like that three week transit getting to South Carolina?

KH: It was awful, Lord, and wonderful at the same time. When they put me in the suicide-watch cell because that was the only open bed, I thought I would die. It was awful being locked in solitary for twenty-three hours a day!

GOD: I know, son; I was with you. You didn't die, did you?

KH: No, God, I made it, but sleeping on that concrete slab was real uncomfortable and hurt my back. I was so lonely.

GOD: I know a lot about back pain, son. I know about loneliness as well. I was with you.

KH: I know, God, the fellowship was so sweet. I feel like I know You now better than ever before in my life. I learned a lot. Why did you let them do that to me, Lord? Why solitary confinement?

GOD: Have any other people in history ever been locked up in solitary confinement like that?

KH: Probably millions have, Lord. I shudder to think of all the pain man has inflicted on his fellow man over the centuries!

GOD: Son, you wouldn't believe me if I told you all that I've seen man do to his fellow man! Now that you have been through that trial, do you notice an automatic kindred-spirit bonding when you meet someone else who has been through that?

KH: Yes, Lord. It's amazing! Our shared suffering immediately opens a door for me to witness. Is that why you allowed that?

GOD: You are catching on, son—a little slow sometimes, but there is hope. When they took you from Marianna to Pensacola and then back to Tallahassee, you were shackled and chained for six and a half hours straight. Did you like that?

KH: No, Lord. It was awful! My wrists and ankles hurt bad for a long time afterwards. Why did you allow that?

GOD: Son, do you feel more compassion now for all prison inmates who have suffered that treatment?

KH: Oh, yes, Lord, I do! No one should be treated like that!

GOD: Do you see why my perfect law (Psalms 19:7) allowed for beatings (Deuteronomy 25), fines (Exodus 22), and death (Exodus 21:12), but never prison?

KH: Yes, Lord, I do. The more I meditate in your law (Psalms 1:2), the more I see of your great wisdom.

Why On Earth Did God Let This Happen... For Heaven's Sake?

GOD: As for your feet and ankles, son, you should see what they did to Joseph's feet in Egypt (Psalms 105:18) or Paul's feet (Acts 16:24). They were watching you, son, and whispering to each other saying, "Yes, that hurts him, but you should have seen my ankles." You all can swap war stories when you get up here. They are cheering for you as well. Paul says to keep running the race! Finish your course (II Timothy 4:7)! Your dad and mom, your father-in-law, your first three children, your son-in-law, and a lot of others are cheering you on, son.

> *Trust me. I built this place up here. It will be well worth all the minor problems you face down there (II Corinthians 4:17). I'll wipe away all tears, son (Revelation 21:4).*
>
> *By the way, that experience made you a "brother" to many millions of men and women. Now you can better minister to them as well. Joseph carried scars on his feet for life, but the experience made him a kinder father and husband and prepared him to be a great ruler. He says hello as well.*

KH: Thanks, God. Tell him hello for me. I love reading his story. It is a real source of strength and encouragement to me.

GOD: Your story is encouraging a lot of people too, son. Even some outspoken atheists and evolutionists are rethinking their rejection of Me based on what has happened to you this past year.

KH: But, Lord, my reputation has been destroyed!

GOD: First, son. I made myself of no reputation for you (Philippians 2:7). Second, none of that will matter when you all face Me. Third, let Me handle that stuff, son. Quit griping and win souls.

KH: Okay, Lord. I'm sorry. I'll try. Lord, when you sent me to the Tallahassee prison for a week, no one got saved. Why did you send me?

GOD: Mike was there, son. He's been saved for many years but was taught in his church that he could lose his salvation. When he was arrested two years ago, he got bitter at me. He thought he had lost his salvation and hadn't spoken to Me since his arrest. He talked with you there for several hours. Do you remember that?

KH: Yes, Lord. I remember. He did seem to get a glow of hope when I explained salvation is a gift from you and that he cannot lose it.

GOD: It is a lot more than a glow, son. He is fired up and praying to Me all the time now. He will serve Me for many years. His life will touch hundreds for My kingdom. Was a week in a Tallahassee prison worth changing hundreds of lives?

KH: Yes, Lord, of course. I had no idea.

GOD: I told you, son, you have no idea about a lot of things. Quit complaining and trust me.

KH: Okay, Lord. I'm trying.

GOD: How did you like the prison holding unit in Atlanta, son?

KH: It was terrible, Lord! Worse than the suicide-watch cell in many ways. The food was bad and never enough. I lost five pounds in eight days. They have three men in a 7' x 14' room for twenty-three hours a day. The rooms are designed for two, but I wouldn't keep a dog in one overnight. I never saw the sun for eight days.

GOD: You needed to lose a few pounds, son. How do you feel?

KH: I feel great, Lord! I only led one man to you, Lord. We only got out for one hour a day to shower, see the counselor, clean the room and change the laundry.

GOD: Yes, son, the man was Lavan. Pretty tall, wasn't he?

KH: Yes, Lord! Seven foot one! The biggest man I have ever witnessed to.

GOD: He seemed eager to trust Me didn't he, son?

KH: Yes, Lord. When I told him I was an evangelist, he lit up and said, "I wish I could be a Christian!" He was "ripe" for the pickin'. I couldn't explain it fast enough for him. He prayed in fifteen minutes and really seemed genuine. Did I go too fast, Lord? I worry about converts like that.

GOD: No, son. He was just real ready to accept Me as his only hope of heaven. His mother has been praying for him without ceasing (I Thessalonians 5:17). He has eleven children. He has been selling drugs and ruining lives for years. When he gets out in fourteen months, he will be a new man. Those quick Bible study tips you gave him and his Christian cell mate will help him grow. His children will all be tall and natural "kid magnets." With dad's new godly influence, many will come to me. You did what I wanted, son.

> *I'll show you the results one day. Trust me. As for not seeing the sun for eight days, how many people have experienced that?*

KH: Probably millions, Lord.

GOD: My daughter Fanny Crosby was blind from age six weeks until she died at age ninety-five. She never saw the sun. How would you like that, son?

KH: That would be awful, Lord.

GOD: She wrote eight thousand songs to praise Me during those years, son. She sees fine now and is also watching you. I thought eight days would be enough to help you understand. By the way, son, where are you now?

KH: Lord, I'm outside enjoying Your glorious sunshine on a gorgeous day in South Carolina. I really need the sunshine for my health. Thank you, Lord! What is my next assignment while I'm here?

Why On Earth Did God Let This Happen... For Heaven's Sake?

GOD: One step at a time, son. I'll guide you. What happened after lunch today?

KH: I was sitting in the sun writing to you and Don came over and sat down to talk. He sure was eager to learn about the Bible. He gladly asked You to forgive his sins and trusted You as Savior.

GOD: Yes, I was there with you. Don is twenty-seven years old. His life will do a complete 180^0 turn during the next twenty months in prison. I have big plans for him, son. Thanks for being obedient to my leading, son. Sometimes, I have a hard time getting you to listen to me.

KH: I know, Lord. Sorry about that. I have another question, Lord. Why did you let them them move me five hundred miles away from my family? I was not in any trouble in the Pensacola Camp. I worked extra hard at every job I was given.

GOD: Do you remember how Joseph's brothers sold him into slavery?

KH: Yes, Lord.

GOD: They meant it for evil, but I used it for good (Genesis 50:20): didn't I?

KH: Yes, Lord, You did.

GOD: So the motives of those who sold him really don't matter do they, son? You did nothing wrong to deserve the move as a punishment. The move was purely political, but you will see why I allowed all this one day.

KH: Lord, When I finally got here in South Carolina, I discovered fifteen men from the Pensacola Camp had just arrived the week before. I couldn't believe all the false rumors they had heard about why I was moved! All I knew was that it was ordered by another inmate's judge because we are both appealing IRS cases. I don't see why we need to be separated. We have different judges and different issues. Why did you allow them to move me, Lord?

GOD: You were in Pensacola for two months, son. I was done with you there. This move is all part of my plan for your life. Forget the rumors. You should have heard all the rumors about me during my time on earth! You do right and let them talk. I know this is hard for you. How many men in there are away from their families?

KH: Nearly all of them, Lord. Some only see their families once a year—and some not at all. I know what you are going to say, Lord, that now I know how they feel and can be a better witness to them, right?

GOD: Very good, son. You are starting to get the picture!

KH: But, Lord, five hundred miles away?

GOD: You are still in America, son. Would you prefer...Siberia?

KH: Oh, no, South Carolina is just fine! Hey, Lord, why did you let me slip on those steps in Atlanta and bruise my ankle so badly?

GOD: I needed you to see the new prison doctor that just came from India. He knows almost nothing about Me, son. I know you didn't have much time with him, but you did tell him about your Website. He will look at it and read the "How To Be Saved" article. That will start him on the road to salvation later this year.

> *I'm sorry about the bruise, but you can't see the doctor in there unless you are hurt. Would you rather I break it next time—or bruise your head?*

KH: No, Lord! The ankle was a great idea. I have one more question, Lord.

GOD: Yes, son, and I know what it is. You want to know when you will get out of prison, don't you?

KH: Yes, Lord. I sure do.

GOD: Son, when Daniel went into the den of lions, did he know when or even if he would come out alive?

KH: No, Lord.

GOD: Did Shadrach and his friends know when they would come out of the furnace?

KH: I don't think so, Lord.

GOD: Did Noah know how long the Flood would last when he went into the ark? Did Abraham know how long he would wait for the promised child? Did Moses know how long it would take to lead those stubborn Jews to the Promised Land?

KH: I doubt it, Lord. None of them knew how long it would take?

GOD: Don't you want to experience what these heroes of the faith experienced so that you can bond with them when you get up here?

KH: Well..... If that's what you think is best, Lord.

GOD: It is best, son. I know this is a tough assignment, but I never give out more than you can bear (I Corinthians 10:13). By the way, son, this experience has humbled you and our relationship is much closer.

> *Job never knew when or even if his test would end, but he is fine now. He says, "Hang in there, Kent! I know how you feel!"*
>
> *Son, if I told you when you were getting out, these guys up here would all say, "Hey God, You never told us!" That might start a riot up here, son! I'm sorry, but you will have to wait like everyone else.*

KH: But Lord, I miss my family so badly!

GOD: Those men you are with all miss their families, too, son. Your family is fine. I'm watching over them. You will be back with them. Son, lots of people are watching you.

You are helping people who are not in prison by your being in prison. You are doing my will, son. You just need to do one more thing for me.

KH: I know—quit griping!

GOD: You got it, son! You catch on slowly, but there is hope.

KH: Thanks for your patience, Lord.

GOD: Son, I've given you a wide variety of cell mates as part of your training. You've had to live with big ones, little ones, loud, obnoxious ones and quiet ones. I put you in with Muslims, Catholics, Jehovah's Witnesses, Jews, Baptists, Buddhists, Nazis, communists, pagans, Wiccans, Methodists, Mormons, and Lutherans.

> *You have lived with African Americans, Asians, Caucasians, Hispanics, Native Americans, and every mix in between. You've seen a wide variety of lifestyles, personalities, diets, beliefs, and various degrees of bodily cleanliness. You have slept on concrete, steel, old bags of cotton, blue foam pads, and two-inch mattresses.*
>
> *You have been real cold, real hot, and just right. You've had good food, bad food, boring food, and no food. In short, son, I have let you get a royal education in a short time.*
>
> *You have experienced the twenty-two man pod, the twelve-man crowded room, solitary lockdown, two-man cells with eight-hour lockdown, two-man cells with three in it with twenty-three-hour lockdown, and now, the one-hundred-thirty-man open dorm with three-man cubicles. Which do you like best?*

KH: I'll take my short, Scotch-Irish wife with her sweet smile, sweet spirit, good cooking, and good looks, my own bed, my children and grand-children and my ministry.

GOD: I understand, son. All the men with you want to go home as well. Will you be a better husband, father, and preacher because of all of this?

KH: I think so, Lord. This has been good for me in thousands of ways. I think I have learned a lot! But I want to go home!!

GOD: I know, son. Home will come. Be patient.

KH: I'm trying, Lord. What's up for tomorrow?

GOD: We've been over that before, son. One day at a time—I'll guide you. Go to sleep.

KH: Okay, Lord. Good night. Thank you for being so awesome!

GOD: Good night, son. I'll be here when you need me. I never sleep (Psal 121:4).

KNEE-MAIL CONVERSATION BETWEEN GOD AND SIMON THE ZEALOT
June 19, 2007
(written from the Federal Prison Camp Edgefield, South Carolina. Based on Luke 6:15; Acts 1:13)

GOD: Simon, you don't seem happy. What's wrong?

Simon: (Simon the Zealot): I don't understand some things, Lord.

GOD: Well, let's hear it, Simon.

Simon: I'm a patriotic Israelite, Lord. I love my country and our great heritage. We are slaves to the Romans, Lord, and I don't like it. My fellow Zealots and I are the only ones offering real resistance to the Romans. We sneak out at night and blow up bridges, loosen chariot-wheel lug nuts, and change road signs to disrupt the enemy. I've followed you for several years now, hoping you would restore our great nation by leading a revolt against the Romans. But you don't show any interest in helping free Israel from oppression.

I've put up with the likes of Matthew the Roman tax collector as a soul-winning partner several times. I wondered why you invited him to join our group of disciples. I first thought maybe you did that to have an insider in the Roman camp to feed you information. Over the years I kept watching to see if you would rebuke him for betraying his country and working with the hated Romans, but you never have. It's as if you don't even care that he was actually assisting the enemy before he joined us.

I don't understand, Lord. When do we fight and kick the Romans out of our land (Acts 1:6)?

GOD: I'm the one who founded Israel, son. I'm the original patriot. I love this land and desire the best for Israel more than you can ever know. I also have seen everything the Romans have done and already know everything they will do and even what they think. I don't need an insider to feed me information. (Isaiah 66:18; Matthew 9:4, 12:25; Luke 5:22; Hebrews 4:12)

As for fighting to rid our land of the Romans, I don't need your help to do that, Simon. Did you see what just one of my angels did in II Kings 19:35 to the Assyrians?

Simon: Yes, Lord. He killed 185,000 of their top soldiers in one night.

GOD: He was just an ordinary angel, so can you imagine what twelve legions of them could do (Matthew 26:53)?

Simon: That is hard to fathom, Lord. I bet they could destroy all of Israel's enemies in a few seconds!

GOD: Yes, they could, Simon, but the greatest enemy Israel has would still be there.

Simon: Who is that, Lord? I can't imagine an enemy worse than the Romans. They are heathens!

GOD: Their hearts are wicked, son. The problem is not Rome. The enemy of the Israelites is their own hearts! It is the enemy we've been working on for several years now. Yes, many lives have been changed, yet Israel's worst enemy still lies within.

Simon: Yes, Lord, I have seen thousands of lives changed, but yes, I acknowledge there remains great wickedness in the hearts of the people.

GOD: As long as Israel is wicked, I will be their enemy, Simon (Psalm 7:11). Getting rid of the Romans wouldn't fix that problem. You and your fellow Zealots could kill every Roman and the real problem would still remain. Don't you remember what I told Jeremiah to preach to Israel?

Simon: Yes, Lord. You told him to tell Israel not to fight against Nebuchadnezzar. You said that you had sent the King of Babylon to punish Israel (Jeremiah 28:14).

GOD: Yes, Simon. I told him that wicked Nebuchadnezzar was my servant (Jeremiah 25:9). I told Nebuchadnezzar to destroy Israel. That was not the time for patriots, Simon. No amount of guerilla warfare would have saved Israel. I had ordered their destruction. They needed a revival, not a revolution.

Simon: Did you send the Romans here, Lord?

GOD: Yes, I did, Simon. I will punish them when I'm done using them just like I did Nebuchadnezzar (Jeremiah 25:12).

The Romans are wicked and evil and need my judgment, but I expect the heathen to be heathen, son. The thing that really bothers me is when my people act like the heathen (II Chronicles 7:14). I will use the wicked Romans to punish my people Israel, and then I will punish the Romans for doing it. Everyone will be treated fairly, son. I don't make mistakes.

Don't misunderstand, son. Sometimes, it is good to defend the land against internal or external enemies. I raised up Moses and Joshua and many judges to free my people from bondage, didn't I?

Simon: Yes, Lord. I read their stories and want to be like them. I'm willing to die for my country, Lord.

GOD: I know you are, Simon, and I appreciate that spirit in you, but this is not the time for patriots. This is the time for prophets and preachers and prayers. Sometimes, it is my will for Israel to be punished by going into slavery.

I'm always willing to forgive and rescue them. I normally raise up a Gideon for occasions like that; but right now, Israel has not repented, so you Zealots are wasting your time. My people often get involved in fights they shouldn't be in. What happened when good King Amaziah got into a fight that he should not have been involved in? (II Chronicles 25:17-25; II Kings 14:9-14).

Simon: He was badly beaten, Lord.

GOD: That's right, Simon. Let me pick the battles.

Simon: But Lord, what about Matthew? Isn't he a traitor?

GOD: I called him to follow me and he did (Matthew 9:9). Did you hear what my prophet John the Baptist told the publicans to do to show they had repented (Luke 3:12-13)?

Simon: Yes, Lord, he told them not to cheat the people by collecting more than the law allowed.

GOD: He didn't tell them to quit their job, did he, Simon?

Simon: No God, he didn't.

GOD: Did he tell the Roman soldiers to quit their jobs?

Simon: No, Lord. He just told them to do violence to no man and to be content with their wages.

GOD: Like Solomon said, there is a time for everything. There are times to fight for freedom and there are times to refrain from fighting (Ecclesiastes 3:1). Right now is not the time to be a patriot. Israel's judgment is coming soon. They are like rebellious Ephraim. "Ephraim is joined to idols. Let him alone" (Hosea 4:17).

Simon: But God! I love my country and want to see a revival.

GOD: So do I, Simon. Israel has been through this cycle many times. They never seem to learn. They go from prosperity to complacency to sin to judgment to repentance and back to prosperity. Right now, they need my judgment, son. Trust me, it is best. All countries and people seem to follow the same vicious cycle. One day I will help a group of godly men found a great country called America. They will become very prosperous and then very wicked. I will send them thousands of bureaucrats and princes to eat all their substance and bring them into bondage (I Samuel 8:10-18; Proverbs 28:2). I will call on my prophets to stop trying to save their nation and just win souls before my judgment falls. You will see it all from Heaven, Simon, and it will break your heart as it does mine.

Simon: What should I do, Lord?

GOD: Quit the Zealots. Submit to the Romans. Love your enemies. Bless them that curse you (Matthew 5:44). Preach my gospel to all the world (Mark 16:15).

Simon: Okay, Lord, if that is what you think is best.

GOD: I always know what is best, son.

KNEE-MAIL CONVERSATION BETWEEN GOD AND KENT ON PSALM 23 AND NUMBERS
June 26, 2007
(written from the Federal Prison Camp Edgefield, South Carolina)

KH: Lord, it's me again.

GOD: I know, son, I've been expecting your knee-mail.

KH: Lord, I've been busy for you nearly all thirty-eight years of my Christian life. I like being busy!

GOD: I know, son; I know all your works. You should read the seven letters to the seven churches in Revelation 2 and 3. I know everyone's works, son, and I will judge each according to their works (Revelation 20:12).

KH: I know, Lord, and I want to get back to work for You doing the work of an evangelist (II Timothy 4:5). Why are You keeping me in prison?

GOD: You are still doing the work I called you to, son. You are witnessing to people both in and out of the prison right now. Many are encouraged by your blogs.

KH: But Lord, I want to go home.

GOD: I know, son, and you will. I'm almost done with you in there. Be patient. Lots of My children are eager to work for Me, but sometimes, I must make them slow down, sit down, or lie down. Taking time to talk with me is more important than working. You read about Mary and Martha, didn't you (Luke 10:41-42)?

KH: Yes, Lord, many times. Martha was too busy to stop and listen to You. Have I done that, Lord?

GOD: Yes, son, many times. I know you like to work and preach and get things done (Proverb 13:19), but I still have a lot of things I want to teach you. I'm the Shepherd, you will not want (Psalm 23). I'll provide all your needs, not wants (Philippians 4:19), take care of your family, and make you lie down in green pastures all at the same time.

KH: But, Lord, I don't want to lie down. I feel great! I'm rested, Lord. Can I go back to work now?

GOD: When I'm done, son. Sheep need to be forced to rest and digest once in a while. You do too. I know you are rested, but there are many things in My

Word you have not seen yet. Sheep have to re-chew things they have already chewed and swallowed. You have read Psalm 23 many times, son, but you missed a lot! Count the references to Me in there.

KH: Wow! That's cool, Lord!

Verse one says "the Lord" one time.
Verse two says "He" or "His" twice.
Verse three says "He" three times.
Verse four says "Thou" or "Thy" three times.
Verse five says Thou" two times.
Verse six says "the Lord" one time.

I never saw that, Lord. You are in there twelve times, and the Psalm begins and ends with You!

GOD: Now count the pronouns David used to refer to My meeting his needs.

KH: There are seventeen, Lord.

GOD: That's correct, son. Count the times "sheep" is used in John 10:1-30.

KH: There are seventeen, Lord! That's cool!

GOD: Read Acts 2, son, and see how many languages got the Gospel on that one day.

KH: It's seventeen again, Lord! What does it all mean?

GOD: I want the whole world saved, son (II Peter 3:9). Those seventeen language groups are symbolic of the entire world. Write down the numbers 1 - 17, son. What is the middle number?

KH: It's nine, Lord.

GOD: Now add all seventeen numbers.

KH: Wow! They all add up to 153! That's how many fish were in the net in John 21:11!!

GOD: Yes, son. There were 153 countries in the world at the time John wrote that. I will gather of all nations (Isaiah 66:18) into my Kingdom. Now look at the number 153.

What is $(1 \times 1 \times 1) + (5 \times 5 \times 5) + (3 \times 3 \times 3)$?

KH: Wow! It is 153 again!

GOD: What is 9 x 17?

KH: It's 153 again! I wondered why you bothered to record the number of fish they caught. Now I see.

GOD: You are too busy, son. I made you lie down. Keep chewing on My Word, son. There is more stuff in there than you can imagine! Just search out where seventeen appears again in My Word and see how I provide for My sheep (Genesis 37:2; 47:28, etc.). Now search the word "still." It's important that the sheep get still waters, son. I calmed the waters (Mark 4:39) because they needed still waters that day as well. I am restoring your soul to make you more effective as a husband, a father, a grandfather, a boss, a neighbor, and an evangelist. You were bearing fruit, son, but when I get done pruning, you will bear much fruit (John 15:2). Did you notice the word "leadeth" is used twice?

KH: Yes, Lord.

GOD: There are several kinds of leading, son. The first one is leading someone who is willing and wanting to be led. That's the kind in verse two. The second is leading someone who does not want to go. I often have to lead people in paths of righteousness who are reluctant to go there like Balaam in Numbers 22:24.

I do this "for My name's sake." I will be glorified in all the earth. Sometimes people who like to be busy, like you, need to be made to lie down for a while. I told Elijah to go to the brook and wait until I told him what to do. While there, one of the greediest birds on earth, the raven, provided all his needs for food. Despite the source of your provision, you have food and housing provided for you, don't you, son?

KH: Yes, Lord. The food is great. The conditions are not bad, but I want to go home!

GOD: I know, son. I'll send you home when I'm ready. You have been in high gear most of your life. You need to just sit and talk with me. We have talked a lot these last nine months, haven't we, son?

KH: Yes, Lord, the fellowship has been sweet.

GOD: There are many sides to a diamond, son. Each one gets cut and polished separately. I've been polishing another side of you, so I can use you to reflect My glory more. I know what I'm doing. Relax, sit still, and enjoy My company. I'll take care of everything, son. Don't worry. For now, lie still while I polish.

KNEE-MAIL BETWEEN GOD AND KENT ON, 'HOW MUCH LONGER?'
July 11, 2007

KH: I'm sure weary of being in prison, Lord. How much longer?

GOD: There is no hurry, son. I'm in charge and I don't get worried, concerned, or nervous. I see the end from the beginning. Everything will be OK.

KH: God, can You at least tell me why You allowed this. I tried so hard to obey the laws about taxes and still feel that both I and the ministry have been wronged. Now my sweet little wife faces prison as well. It's so unfair, Lord! Especially for her!

GOD: What did your dad teach you to do with complex problems or questions, son?

KH: He taught me to list all the options we could think of and then study and pray about the list. All ideas, even the dumb ones, were put on the list. You always seemed to show us the truth that way.

GOD: That was great advice he gave you, son (Proverbs 4:1). What ideas have you had about this problem? Why did this happen to you?

KH: As you well know, Lord, I've thought about it for many hours now. Here is my list so far:

1. *I broke some law that no one, not even the IRS, has been able to show me yet.*
2. *I was proud in Your work and needed to be humbled (Proverbs 16:18).*
3. *You are done using me and I'm being set aside (I Corinthians 9:27).*
4. *This is training for an even greater ministry ahead.*
5. *I needed time off to recharge and get closer to You (I Kings 17:3).*
6. *There were people in the six places I've been to whom You wanted me to testify about You.*
7. *You and Satan were discussing me like Job and all this is a test for You to show Satan what a loser he is again. This time, I get to be Job (Job 2:2-6).*
8. *The agents, legal staff, prison personnel, judges, or someone in the food chain is being tested by You to see how they would handle Your children when they were given a chance. King Herod, Pilate, Pharoah, Hitler, Stalin, Mao, Pol Pot, Roe vs. Wade Supreme Court Justices, and thousands of others have failed similar tests down through time (Psalms 105:15).*
9. *You wanted to show me how corrupt our legal system is; so I'll understand when You bring judgement on America (Psalms 9:17).*

10. *This happened to give me time to read all the books by Dr. Gill, Richard Wurmbrand, Henry Morris, Ray Comfort, Tommy Tenney, and scores of others that have changed me forever.*
11. *This happened to give me time to watch all the videos by T.D. Jakes, Moody, Billy Graham, Charles Stanley, and dozens of others that have further changed me for good, I hope.*
12. *This happened to allow my son, my family, and my staff at CSE a chance to trust You more and grow closer to You.*
13. *This happened to show us that You can supply for us even through this very difficult and expensive trial (Philippians 4:19).*
14. *This happened to allow thousands to hear about your Word through the negative press and Web sites that blast me daily. This causes many to say, "Who is this guy they hate so badly?" Many search and find our videos and end up getting saved and supporting our ministry!*
15. *This happened to see if some of Your children would judge me without knowing all the information (Proverbs 18:13; Matthew 7:2).*
16. *This happened to give me time to write books and research for new videos that will win souls to You.*
17. *This happened to meet and make friends with hundreds of drug dealers, thieves, and convicts who will help me, my family, Your ministry, or the cause of Christ during the coming bad times (Luke 16:9).*
18. *This happened to see the evil done by the unconstitutional "conspiracy laws" passed by Reagan (Matthew 24:10).*
19. *This happened to see how wise our founding fathers were to restrict the federal government to Washington, D.C., forts, and post offices.*
20. *This happened to see how far America has gone astray from that plan.*
21. *This happened to see how Your children did not seek Your face when pushing to elect judges and congressmen who promise to be "tough on crime" by giving out huge prison sentences which are indeed "burdens grievous to be born" (Luke 11:46)—when they don't have a clue what even thirty days in prison does to a man, his family, and society, let alone thirty months or thirty years.*
22. *This happened to show me how petty some Bureau of Prisons' staff and correction officers can be, just as predicted in Proverbs 30:22.*
23. *This happened to see the wisdom of I Timothy 6:10 and how some leaders make huge profits off the prison system while millions of children, families, and society in general suffer.*
24. *This happened to let me spend thirty minutes a day getting Vitamin D from the sun to repair the bone damage in my back from that car wreck thirty-five years ago, as I do feel better.*
25. *This happened to show me how dumb it is to make drugs illegal and create this giant criminal element and prison system. Your laws never call for a punishment for possession of anything—only for actions, which*

actually harm someone else.

26. *This happened to let me really meditate on the incredible wisdom found in Your law (Psalm 1:2).*
27. *This happened to meet future workers for Your kingdom.*
28. *This happened to let me hear the horror stories of how innocent men get locked up by our current "injustice system."*
29. *This happened to show me how soon tribulation is coming to the earth and motivate me to do even more.*
30. *This happened to test and try me to make me more like You (Hebrews 2:10).*
31. *This happened to see firsthand how Your Word changes lives in prison!*
32. *This happened to see firsthand the incredible waste of time, energy, money, food, and resources caused by our government.*
33. *This happened to let me see the suffering inflicted on millions by our government, as nearly every other government in history has done.*
34. *This happened to let me experience humiliation, chains, solitary confinement, and all the other things I've seen in prison to make me more compassionate with the millions who have been through this around the world (II Corinthians 1:3-5).*
35. *This happened to lose twenty pounds and get in better physical shape.*
36. *This happened to show me how much I love my wife, family, ministry, and freedom.*
37. *This happened to discover who my real friends and my real enemies are.*
38. *This happened to discover those who say they love Jesus, yet kick me when I'm down. Judas apparently has cousins alive today.*
39. *This happened to show me the dangers of 501 (c) (3) and how most of Your children will compromise during the tribulation over these issues.*
40. *This happened to show me how stupid it is for our courts to be using "case law" where a judge's decision can overturn the obvious reading of the Constitution, as well as common law.*
41. *This happened to let me see the well organized tool room in Pensacola for ideas for our ministry.*
42. *This happened to give me experience in a commercial kitchen to prepare me for CSE to have a creation campground some day.*
43. *This happened to see that some men who have been here for ten years are still profane, thieves, liars, and adulterers at heart. I see now that even after 1,000 years, Satan will still be unchanged (Revelation 20:7-10).*
44. *This happened to be a testimony to some men who had no spiritual training.*
45. *This happened to learn the value of time with my family.*
46. *This happened to have others be motivated to do more for You since I'm locked up (Philippians 1:14).*

47. *This happened to finally have time to practice the piano.*
48. *This happened to have time to sing since I normally saved my voice for preaching.*
49. *This happened to see the damage done to children by the way our prison system works. I cry for my family nearly every day.*
50. *This happened to tenderize my heart for lost souls.*

GOD: That's a good start, son. There are several hundred more things I will accomplish and a few items on your list are not correct; but overall, you are seeing the big picture.

KH: Which ones are not right, Lord?

Satan: I hate to interrupt, but as god of this world (oh how I wish that could be a capital G! [II Corinthians 4:4]), I monitor all knee-mails to protect my interests. There are some obvious reasons you forgot.

1. *You are in God's family and, therefore, you are my enemy. I asked for and received permission to do this to you to destroy your faith in God.*
2. *Thousands have been converted to Christ because of the simple way you expose evolution. I hate people like you who steal people from my kingdom!*
3. *Evolution has been my religion since the Garden of Eden. I want people to believe the lie that they are improving and can one day be a god. Your message destroys that; so I hate you and will stop you any way I can.*
4. *Did you see all the instant bad press about you after the trial? I had my agents ready to jump on this one! Your fall has caused many to reject the creation message and remain in my kingdom.*
5. *Your fall has made my children rejoice! They are much more bold now to spread my message of evolution. Because of your simple answers, many of them had become slack and even had begun to doubt their faith in me. You did much damage to my family; so I decided to damage your family.*
6. *You were encouraging common people to start similar ministries to expose evolution and many were doing it. I don't mind it as much when the super-intellectuals speak on creation because they use all the big words and complex proofs that only a few understand. But your method of making it simple is way too effective (Mark 12:37).*
7. *Your "Questions and Answers Session" on Seminar #7 makes me angry because you explain the King James issue clearly and cause people to doubt all my false Bibles. I have worked hard for six thousand years to make people question or doubt or change God's Words and you are undoing my work. I hate you for this!*
8. *You have also dared to try to take dinosaurs away from me. I have used*

dinosaurs for nearly two hundred years to teach billions of people that the earth is billions of years old and that God's Word is not true. Your seminar on dinosaurs strikes at the heart of my kingdom. I intend to destroy both your ministry and your reputation for good. Dinosaurs are especially effective for me to deceive children. You are taking children away from me, so I took yours away from you!

9. *You have been a fool, Hovind, to follow Jesus. I am the prince of this world (John 14:30). You know you are commanded to submit to those who rule over you (Romans 13 and Hebrew 13). You can clearly see that the state is lord over the church. Stop preaching against evolution and enjoy life with your family. We can peacefully co-exist. You can have your religion. Just leave my kingdom alone. I have plans to rule this entire world (Psalms 2).*

GOD: Son, don't listen to those who darken counsel by words without knowledge (Job 38:2). I told you all things would work together for good if you love me (Romans 8:28). Do you love me, son?

KH: I want to love You, Lord, but if you will mark iniquities (Psalm 130:3) who can stand? I've been reading Your Word, praying, going to church, and witnessing to others for thirty-eight years now, Lord; and all I can see are my failures and sins. The closer I try to get to You, the more I see that I'm vile (Isaiah 6:5)! I don't know how to answer Your question, Lord, except to say that I want to love You!

GOD: I know, son. I search the hearts (I Chronicles 28:9; Romans 8:27; Revelation 2:23). I see your struggles (II Peter 2:7-8). I saved you from the penalty of your sin thirty-eight years ago. I am saving you from the power of sin and one day soon, I will save you from the very presence of sin. Until then, I know about your struggle (Romans 7:18-25).

KH: Thanks for helping me so far, God. You are truly awesome!

GOD: Son, would you love me if I make you serve the entire ten years in prison?

KH: That is sure not my will, God; but I would try.

GOD: What if I need your case to go all the way to the Supreme Court to get a ruling that helps millions? Would you be happy with sitting there for several years while I do this?

KH: Lord, You know my heart. I would not be happy, but I trust You to do right (Genesis 18:25). I would be happy if I could go home with no parol or probation while this case is on appeal. I am happiest when I'm teaching others about Your creation, like I did for seventeen years.

GOD: What if I decide you are more fruitful for me in there? Your blog encourages many and your imprisonment has caused many to be more bold (Philippians 1:12-14). Would you be happy to know your being in prison does more good for My kingdom than your traveling and preaching?

KH: Lord, I love You and want what is best. I also have a deep love for my family, my grandkids, my ministry, and my freedom. Can't I have both? Surely You can make both happen!

GOD: How many people in the Bible lost family for My sake (Mark 10:28-30)?

KH: Hundreds did, Lord. I don't understand it or like it, but I trust Your leadership, Lord. Can I please go home now?

GOD: Son, your case is bigger than you realize. There is a real battle going on between the forces of evil and the forces of good (Daniel 10:13). I see your tears and hear your prayers as well as the prayers of thousands of others.

KH: Lord, I throw myself at the mercy of Your court. You said You would give me the desires of my heart if I delight myself in You (Psalms 37:4). My desire is to go home. This prison time has been good in a thousand ways, but my heart is not here. You know my desire; now please show me how to delight in You and honor Your Word and send me home, please.

GOD: I love you, son. I will do what is best.

KH: Lord, when I read how they tortured Richard Wurmbrand in "In God's Underground," I felt like such a wimp here. I get three good meals a day, a clean place to sleep, hot showers, Christian fellowship, lots of mail, my Bible, exercise, sunshine, an easy job, letters to and from my family, freedom to witness and no beatings. Your children have been badly mistreated for two thousand years now. Why do You allow this? Please come back soon, Lord! I can't wait to see Satan cast into hell. Can I please push the button or pull the lever or whatever opens the door for him to be thrown in?

GOD: There is a l-o-o-o-n-g list of people who also want that job, son! And son, there are a lot of people both in and out of the prison watching you. Thanks for letting Me use you in this special assignment. I'm proud of you, son. It will be over soon. Be strong.

KH: Thank you, Lord. I'll try.

GOD: Son, would it help you if I told you that My church is about to enter a time when many go to prison and I sent you ahead to show them how to bear up in prison?

KH: Not really, Lord. First, I'm not bearing up very well; and second, millions have done this before me; and even now, many of your children suffer in prisons and do a much better job of praising You while there. I gripe and complain a lot about being here.

GOD: You are right on both counts, son. I do enjoy your knee-mail as do many of My children out there. I've noticed you write more and pray more since I put you there.

KH: I was hoping You would not notice that, Lord. Does that mean that I stay in for a long while?

GOD: I'll do what is best, son.

KH: I know, God; but that's not a real answer.

GOD: That's the answer I've given to nearly all of My children through history, son. That's the best you will get today. You know what to do. Read My Word, pray, witness, and wait on Me. I've got it all under control. It's late, son. Go to sleep.

KH: Good night, Lord.

NABOTH
July 17 2007
(based on 1 Kings 21)

GOD: Still amazed at how it all happened, aren't you, Son? KH: Stunned would be a better word, Lord. What a system! I was arrested, tried, convicted, sentenced and sent to prison before I could blink and I still don't know what I did wrong! I had no warning.

GOD: Come with Me, Son. We will go visit some folks who know exactly how you feel…

KH: Where are we, Lord?

GOD: Ancient Israel, Son. Those two men talking are citizens of Jezreel. They are cousins. Just listen for a few minutes…

Athili (AT): Hey, Jacob, did you hear about what happened to Naboth?

Jacob (JA): No. What happened? He was fine last week when I saw him.

AT: He was arrested, tried, and convicted of blasphemy against God and the king! He is being stoned this afternoon!

JA: That's not possible. I've known Naboth for years. He is a good man and always tries to obey the Lord and the Law. Where did you hear that story?

AT: It's in the Jezreel News Journal. That's a very conservative paper in his own town. I'm sure they wouldn't print anything that was not true. They said there were two witnesses who testified that they heard him. He must be guilty! I can't believe that I was fooled by him all these years too.

JA: I'm sorry, but I still don't believe it. I've known him too long. Did he admit his guilt during his trial?

AT: No. He didn't even testify in his own defense! His son said that he was innocent and was framed by the king and queen themselves! He says that his dad thought the entire trial was a sham proceeding and that for him to even say a word would make their "trial" seem legitimate. He said that under our system of laws the burden of proof was on the accuser to prove he was guilty, not the accused to prove his innocence. That's why he didn't speak.

JA: Who were the witnesses against him?

AT: They were known liars who were men of Belial, but the paper said their stories agreed they heard him blaspheme. It makes me wonder who else is a phony in the church.

JA: I still think the paper is lying as well as the two witnesses. God told us not to bear false witness (Ex. 20:16) and that a false witness should be punished (Deut. 19:16-19).

AT: There is no way the entire jury could be wrong. These jurors were all intelligent, respected members of the community. They heard all the evidence and voted that he was guilty.

JA: They did not hear all the evidence! They never heard Naboth testify. They only heard what the king wanted them to hear. I still smell a rat. Do you know where Naboth's vineyard is?

AT: No. Where?

JA: Right next door to the palace. I bet the king wanted it and Naboth wouldn't sell, and the whole thing is a set up. Everyone fears wicked King Ahab and his extra wicked wife Jezebel. She is ruthless! I wonder if any of the town elders or jurors in the trial were threatened or intimidated by them somehow. Powerful politicians have been known to do that kind of thing, you know.

AT: I can't believe you would say that! We live in the greatest nation on earth. God Himself told Samuel to anoint King Saul and King David. The king's heart is in the hands of the Lord (Pro. 21:1). There is no way God would let them do any wrong. I'm going to believe the system of justice God gave us. And I trust the paper.

JA: I'm going to watch and see if they try to seize Naboth's property next. That will reveal a lot to me!

Next Day

JA: Hey Athili! Look at this memo I found in the trash last night.

AT: What does it say?

JA: It's from Queen Jezebel to the elders of Jezreel:

To the esteemed elders of Jezreel: If you love your country now is the time to stand up! One of your very own respected citizens, a friend and neighbor to all of you, has committed a grievous sin that must be dealt with swiftly and severely. Naboth has blasphemed both God and the king in violation of Exodus

22:28. He must be dealt with publicly so all will fear God and the King. Naboth is one of those crazy patriots who believe we are still governed by God's Law and the covenant made with King David and King Solomon. He has no respect for the authority of the current king that God has raised up to rule the land. We all know that the word and wishes of the king is the highest law. Naboth is a threat to our national security. Imagine the chaos if his wild ideas of old fashioned patriotism spread! I am sending two of my most trusted servants with this top secret memo. They will testify that they heard Naboth blaspheme with their own ears and saw him do it with their own eyes! Please receive them on my behalf, and be sure to point out Naboth to them when the trial starts.

Elder Caleb: Dear Queen Jezebel, We received your note. We understand what you want and will certainly do as you say. We don't want any trouble with the king or queen as the God ordained rulers of our land. We do have a minor concern though. If these men are to testify that they saw Naboth do this, why do we need to point him out to them?

Queen Jezebel: I'm sorry, that was a slip on my part. Of course they know him, but we can't be too cautious on matters like this. We need to be sure that we convict the right man. We certainly wouldn't want to condemn an innocent man!

Elder: Yes, Your Highness. Consider it done as you wish.

JA: See! I told you I smelled a rat!

KH: God, why do You allow this injustice to go on?

GOD: I knew you would ask. Here is a copy of the note I gave Naboth as he sits in prison awaiting execution:

Dear Naboth,
(based on 1 Kings 21:1-26; 2 Kings 9:21-26)

I heard your prayer asking why all this happened to you. I know you are stunned by the great injustice that has been done. Please allow Me to explain a few things to help you.

1. *You have done nothing wrong, Naboth. This is not a punishment for some secret sin as reported in the papers.*
2. *You did what was right. The vineyard was an inheritance and is for your family forever (Lev. 25:23-28). It was not to be sold.*

3. *Ahab has power as king. His wicked wife has power as queen. People need rulers. They are ordained by Me (Rom. 13). People in positions of power have a great temptation to become proud and corrupt. They are used to getting what they want when they want it. It is a sad fact of life that power corrupts and absolute power corrupts absolutely.*
4. *Ahab and Jezebel did the wrong. They coveted your property in violation of Exodus 20:17. They lied in violation of verse 16. Next they will commit murder in violation of verse 13. They willingly rejected your words that I had forbidden you to sell the land (1 Kings. 21:3).*
5. *I keep careful records, Naboth. I will deal with them severely (2 Kings. 9:26)!*
6. *You and your sons will suffer and die because of their sins.*
7. *Fear not. Millions of innocent people have and will suffer for the sins of others. You see it all through history from Abel, the prophets, Jesus, the 11 disciples, to people under Hitler, Stalin, Pol Pot, Islam, the Inquisition and the list goes on for miles. Don't worry, I will richly reward those who suffer for righteousness sake (Mt. 5:11). I have it all recorded.*
8. *I know it looks unfair to the righteous now, but you haven't seen it from My side yet. I'm working on a much bigger picture! All of this life is a job interview for the real life to come. Your earthly time is nothing compared to eternity (Rom. 8:18).*
9. *Ahab pouted when he could not get his way. All spoiled brats do that.*
10. *Jezebel had complete confidence that her corrupt political system could convict an innocent man (1 Kings. 21:7), and it did. You had no chance of winning in her court. She is one of those rulers that tries to rule without paying attention to My laws. I'll take care of it, Naboth.*
11. *Rulers like Jezebel will lie, make up evidence, and intimidate to get their way. Winning is everything to them (1 Kings 21:8-10)...For now.*
12. *The average jury member will believe their own government officials rather than their own neighbors they have known for years. Few have the courage to stand up to the system.*

Don't be disheartened, Naboth. I have perfect records. Your name will be famous among billions for the next 2,800 years in My Word as well as in the 1,000 year kingdom and then on into eternity. You did what was right, Son. Rest in that. I've got your back.

KH: Thanks, Lord. I worry too much, don't I?

GOD: Yes, you do, Son. Relax. I'll take care of it all.

A DAY IN THE PRISON LIFE OF KENT HOVIND
July 18, 2007

6:00 am Awoke after a good night's sleep

6:10 - 6:30 am Ate breakfast of toast, ham, hot grits, banana, and milk

6:30 - 7:40 am Had the 25' x 30' chapel room to myself to read my Bible, pray, play the piano, and sing to the Lord

7:40 - 8:00 am Walked back to room about 100 yards away to clean for the weekly inspection

8:00 - 8:15 am Read in Flyboys by James Bradley while rooms were inspected

8:15 - 9:15 am Helped a fellow inmate who is a good friend and huge black man with his math as he prepares for his GED

9:15 - 10:00 am Went outside to picnic area to read mail and write responses. Because I have about thirty letters to answer, I decided to write this "Day in the Life..." as a generic response to mail and to update friends and enemies of my life here.

10:00 am Listened as "Yard Recall" was announced over the PA system, which means we all go back to the dorms for all the inmates to be counted, and then to be called out for lunch in the order of the cleanest dorm first to last. My dorm, D-2, is typically second or third. Some of these guys didn't have a mom like I had to teach them to clean. There are four dorms in this camp housing about 140 men each.

10:00 - 10:40 am Relaxed in dorm reading and writing and drinking my three-times-a-week coffee — and I know about that causing babies to be born naked!

10:40 - 11:00 am Waited ten to twenty minutes in line for lunch.

The weather here is gorgeous! About 100 of the guys seem to be Christians, so there is a lot of good fellowship standing in line or walking around the one-third mile track or sitting in the open pavilion at the picnic tables. This camp has a nice baseball field, basketball court, four handball courts, ten treadmills or exercise bikes, a ping-pong table, a small but well-stocked law library, regular library, and chapel library with lots of good videos and books. We also have a barbershop, snack machines, dentist and doctor, and a commissary "store" where we "shop" once a week for items from cake to tennis shoes, ice cream to glasses.

There are no fights or violent incidents of any kind here. Everyone, well almost everyone, is friendly and tries to get along. Many men spend their free time in recreation, exercise, walking, taking classes, reading, talking, or watching TV. There are six TVs in each dorm's TV-viewing room. All are set to different channels and everyone listens with their own radio headphones.

We have six different Christian services or Bible studies every week and a Christian volleyball game on the other day. We also have a Christian movie every Sunday night with snacks at intermission.

Every man has a job here. About twenty of the men walk next door to the warehouse to work every day for Unicore. They pack and ship bulletproof vests for police and military. About seventy of the men go next door to work in the other warehouse that provides food for both our camp and the medium security prison with 1,500 men next door. Some of the men also work at "Facilities" to provide services like ground maintenance, welding, and the powerhouse. Other men like me, work in the kitchen or have various jobs in the camp.

Today, like most days, rather than stand in line to eat, I went into the chapel to watch thirty minutes of T.D. Jakes' incredible message, "He Knows Where You Are." I had heard of T.D. Jakes before but had never heard him preach until last week. I differ with some of his theology, but so far, his powerful preaching has been a real blessing to me.

11:20 am Went last in line to eat, a BLT sandwich - very good!

11:30 - 12:00 am Worked with our four-man crew in the 20' x 30' dish room fast and furiously to clean up from lunch, disassemble and clean the giant dishwashing machines, and clean the floor, done and out the door by 12:02 p.m.

12:02 - 12:07 pm Ran to the dorm to change to my jogging shorts and eat my almost daily Snickers bar—my almost only vice. Ha!

12:10 - 12:40 pm Took time to sunbathe behind the library, fifteen minutes on each side to absorb Vitamin D.

During this time I consider the ants, the ravens, and the lilies as commanded in the Bible. I consider my goals in life like the ant, the way God always provides food as for the raven, and the way God always provides clothes as for the lily. I also consider the heavens as in Psalm 8. It is a warm, partly cloudy, breezy day. If God can make the wind, clouds, atmosphere, sun, stars, and more, He can watch over me in here and you out there!

12:40 - 1:10 pm Walked the track and talked with a Christian brother about the things of God and prayed for my family and staff.

1:10 - 1:45 pm Played the piano and taught another inmate, Earl, basic music theory and how to read a little music. By the end of our session, he could pick out "America the Beautiful" and was so excited!

1:45 - 2:30 pm Studied in the library, reading encyclopedias to learn more and get ideas for my seminar and Dinosaur Adventure Land.

2:35 - 2:50 pm Walked to dorm for a shower. In the shower I shave, brush teeth, wash hair, sing "This World Is Not My Home," and pray for those being persecuted for their faith around the world. The shower reminds me of Hitler's gassing the Jews.

2:50 - 3:20 pm Went back to my "room" to read another chapter in Flyboys and rest. Some days I get a ten-to-fifteen-minute power nap.

3:20 pm Dressed for work

3:26 pm Reported for work again

3:30 - 3:40 pm Set up machines for work

3:40 - 4:00 pm Read and wrote

4:00 - 4:20 pm Ate an early supper of fried chicken, beans, rice, and cake. Read a little more in Flyboys, a great book!

4:20 - 6:30 pm Worked fast and furiously again in the dish room. The waste of food here is incredible!

6:30 pm Got out of kitchen just in time for mail call.

6:35 - 7:05 pm Read carefully and tearfully all twelve of the letters I got tonight. In my nine months in prison, I've only had a few negative letters. Hundreds have been so encouraging and supportive! It is a joy to know so many are praying for me and especially for my wife. Proverbs 25:25!

The sentencing guidelines called for zero to six months probation for her. The judge called the Sentencing Commission in Washington, D.C. and they also told her zero to six months probation was appropriate, but she chose to sentence Jo to one year and one day in Federal Prison. Unless a Stay or Appeal is granted, she must go to prison on August 31st. The judge also granted Forfeiture of the Church Ministry property to pay the amount that was claimed by the Prosecution to have been "structured." This Forfeiture is based on Title 21 drug laws! Our attorneys are working to right this incredible wrong. Please keep praying as this case goes to the 11th Circuit Court of Appeals.

7:05 - 7:45 pm Finished letter to my wife. Jo gets personal letters. Sorry that most of you are only getting "generic letters" right now.

Last Saturday was our 34th anniversary and she was allowed to come visit me! It was great! My daughter and her friend, Paul, came as well. We got to visit both Saturday and Sunday!

I was able to make an attorney call yesterday, the first one in several weeks. He said that the District Judge must rule on one more motion before our case goes to the 11th Circuit. It has been nearly nine months since the end of our trial, at which time we ordered the transcripts. They have still not been produced! The attorneys say that this is unusual and that the 11th Circuit has reprimanded Judge Roger's court twice and fined her once already. Please pray for this issue as well. We cannot file an appeal without the court transcripts.

7:45 pm Went out to walk the track before the 8:00 p.m. prayer meeting, but a thunderstorm stopped that, so I went into the TV room and watched T.D. Jakes' "It's Not in the Field; It's in the House."

9:00 pm Went to walk the track one more time, but stopped to feed the racoon and the fox that come to the fence every night to beg for food.

9:20 pm Heard "Yard recall" announced over the PA, so I came inside to read the CSE blogs' comments sent to me by my office. I wish I could give a personal response to some of those committed evolutionists! When I get out and challenge them to a public debate, watch them quiet down or disappear altogether! Time to organize some of the motions filed in my case. If you have not read the latest motions by my attorney and my wife's attorney (all denied, of course), you should! I do feel a little like Naboth these days (I Kings 21) minus the rocks! God will be sure all issues are judged righteously one day.

10:00 pm Reported for "Count Time" - Everyone must go to their "room" for a counting of all inmates.

10:10 pm Prayed in our prayer circle with a few other Christian brothers.

10:30 pm Finished letters to mail out tomorrow morning when mail is collected at 7:00 a.m.

10:40 pm Read until I was tired and went to sleep.

Thank you for continuing to pray for my release!
Kent

PAY ATTENTION SON!
July 26, 2007

KH: It's me again, Lord.

GOD: I know, son, it's always good to hear from you. I wish you would talk to me more often. I have everything you will ever need or want and more.

KH: I believe You. Lord, it's early in the morning and I want to dedicate this day to You. Is there someone special in here that You want me to reach for You today?

GOD: There is, son. Look in the mirror and you will see him. You are special to Me, and the main person I want to reach through this prison experience is you. It's not what I want you to do. It's what I want you to be.

KH: OK, Lord. Where do we start? I want badly for You to work on me. I seem to have a hard time listening to You.

GOD: Yes, son, I know. You have had a hard time listening since you were a small child. I gave you that hyperactive mind, but you need to get it under better control. Read Luke 10:27; Romans 7:23; 8:7; 12:2; Ephesians 4:23; Philippians 2:5; and I Peter 1:13.

KH: I know, Lord. I'm sorry. I read where You called a lot of people twice to get their attention like "Abraham, Abraham" in Genesis 22:11, "Moses, Moses" in Exodus 3:4, "Samuel, Samuel" in I Samuel 3:10, "Martha, Martha" in Luke 10:41, "Simon, Simon" in Luke 22:31, and "Saul, Saul" in Acts 9:4. It seems like You have to call me hundreds of times to get me to listen.

GOD: That is correct, son. You are what many people call "hard-headed." That can be a good trait if it is used for the right cause (Ezekiel 3:8-9). I can deal with hardheaded better than hard-hearted. You normally don't get too hardhearted (Exodus 14:4,17; Deuteronomy 15:7; I Samuel 6:6; Psalm 95:8; Hebrews 3:8,15). That is good. Keep it that way.

KH: I'll try, Lord. Are you getting tired of working with me yet?

GOD: Not yet, son. I'm merciful, patient, and long suffering (Exodus 34:6). I'll finish what I started in you (Philippians 1:6). Do you remember reading about all the gold items in the tabernacle and temple (Exodus 15:18; 37:7; Numbers 8:4)?

KH: Yes, Lord. I'll bet they were beautiful!

GOD: They are beautiful. You will see them one day. Did you notice how they were formed?

KH: Yes, Lord. They were all beaten into shape.

GOD: That's right, son. I know being in prison makes you feel "beat up" right now, but actually this "beating" is being carefully controlled for your good (Romans 8:28) and My glory (Psalm 8:1). I won't let Satan give you more than you can handle (Job 1:12; 2:6; I Corinthians 10:13).

KH: Lord...I believe You, but it still hurts. I miss my family so badly. We are real close. I still cry for them every day.

GOD: I know, son. I have saved all your tears in a bottle (Psalm 56:8). You will be fine. I'll get you back with them. Where is your faith (Luke 8:25)?

KH: Well...I don't have any trouble with my faith in the past. When I turned down the offer to go to foreman's school at General Motors, I trusted You and I've seen You provide time after time. I trusted You eighteen years ago to start the creation ministry. You have been faithful to protect and provide the whole time.

It's easy to have past faith. I've always seen You after you pass by (Exodus 33:22). I also have future faith, Lord. I believe You will come and rule this world (I Corinthians 15:24-25; Revelation 2:27; 12:5; 19:15).

My problem seems to be with present faith. The current mess I'm in looks pretty bad. I'm locked up; my wife could still go to prison; the judge said the government can seize ministry property to pay for a forfeiture filed against me personally based on drug trafficking laws; we were sentenced on facts that were not presented to the jury, jury instructions were changed after closing arguments, and on the injustices go!

GOD: Your situation is sort of like the disciples in the boat in the storm (Luke 8:23). They were sinking and it looked hopeless.

KH: Exactly! You could have prevented the storm or waited to cross until the next day, but You didn't. Why did You let them almost sink?

GOD: I was with them all the way, son. I wasn't worried at all. I told them we were going over to the other side (Luke 8:22) and we did (Luke 8:26). The little storm in the midst of the trip was to give them a small glimpse of My infinite power. I can do anything! Sometimes My children need to be reminded of that. You do too, son. You preach about Me a lot, but you know so little about Me. I'm with you now!

KH: I know, God. As I have read Your Word these last few weeks, I feel more and more that I know less and less. Though I've read it many times during the past thirty-eight years, it's like a new book to me. I feel so inadequate to do anything for you, Lord.

GOD: That's good, son. Keep it that way. I don't need you to do My work.

KH: I know, Lord, but I need You. I need to do something for You after all You've done for me. I can't wash Your feet with my tears because You aren't here in a body now.

GOD: Oh, yes, I am, son. Read Matthew 25:35-45. You can minister to Me today. I'm all around you. Pay attention!

KH: OK, Lord. I see it now. Thanks!

GOD: Good, son. Get to work. I've got your back.

KENT 2007, KENT 2011 AND MOSES
July 28, 2007

GOD: Good morning, son. I know it's a little early for you (3:00 a.m.) But I wanted to show you something to encourage you. How do like my knee-mail program?

KH: It's amazing, Lord! I can talk directly with you and get answers. Thanks for inventing it.

GOD: Son, you have only seen a very small part of the knee-mail "program" as you call it. Your primitive "World Wide Web" in the twenty-first century is only two-dimensional, and even then it's very limited. Not everyone is connected. My knee-mail is four-dimensional, son, and everyone is connected.

KH: What do you mean, Lord?

GOD: Your two-dimensional Web only operates in the present and can only be accessed by a small percentage of those people living at that time. A 3-D Web would also include up and down features, not just horizontal like you have.

KH: Do you mean with knee-mail, I can access people in Heaven or Hell?

GOD: Yes, and there is much more. You can access using the 4-D feature built into knee-mail. It is not limited by time. You can talk to people in the past, present, or future; but all knee-mail is run through the filter of my incorruptible Word. I don't want to stretch your brain too far this early in the morning, son, but you can knee-mail yourself in the future or past. The only other limitations are that you can't change the past, or see the whole future. Try it, son.

KH: Okay, Lord.

Dear Kent in 2011,

KH 2007: How are you doing?

KH 2011: I'm fine. God has been soooooo good to me. He is awesome. He saw me through all the trials that you are in now and opened up doors to witness of His glory to more people than you would believe. I wish I could tell you when the current trial you are in will end, but information like that is blocked by knee-mail. All I can tell you is that God is too good to give His children more than they can handle (I Corinthians 10:13) and He has things planned for you that you are not capable of processing at this time (I Corinthians 2:9)!

KH 2007: Can you tell me if the IRS seizes the ministry property? They sure want to do that and crush the ministry. The judge gave them permission to seize the assets of Kent

Hovind based on drug laws. How can anyone believe that it is right to seize assets from one entity to satisfy a lien for another? I can't believe the size of the current mess! What happens?

KH 2011: I wish I could tell you, but it is blocked. All I can say is to wait and see what God does! You won't believe it! Remember Moses at the Red Sea when all looked hopeless (Exodus 14:10-12)?

KH 2007: Yes, I do.

KH 2011: Opening up eight miles of nine-hundred-foot deep water so God's children could escape was pretty cool, don't you think?

KH 2007: Yes. I can't wait to see that video when we get to Heaven! I bet even Pharoah was impressed that day!

KH 2011: He was overwhelmed, literally, by it! God is going to work all your current troubles out for your good (Romans 8:28) and for His glory (Psalm 8:1). For now, "Stand still" (Exodus 14:13).

KH 2007: That is so hard for me to do! I'm used to analyzing problems, developing solutions, and fixing things myself. I'm locked up, unable to do anything. This is hard for me.

KH 2011: That's when God does His best work! Moses tried his own way to help his oppressed brothers (Exodus 2:11-12). God had to send him to a forty-year training class on "anger management" in the dessert, and then send him back to do the job God's way. God wants all glory and will not share it with anyone. God will get all glory in your case, Kent. Can I call you "007?"

KH 2007: Sure, that would be fine.

KH 2011: Well then, 007, all you can do now is wait on God to show His mighty arm in your hopeless situation. While you are waiting, I have a suggestion.

KH 2007: Let's hear it.

KH 2011: Do the same thing that Jesus did when he was twelve and had to wait eighteen more years to begin His ministry (Luke 2:52). He worked on all four areas of life: physical, mental, spiritual, and social. Read books, watch good videos, pray, work out, make new friends, and witness to the lost around you. You are right in the middle of a great fishing hole right now. Get fishing for the Master!

KH 2007: I'd rather be out of here fishing somewhere else.

KH 2011: You will be, but for now—wait.

KH 2007: I never liked waiting. As a child, I hated the waiting part of fishing until I discovered bow fishing! I loved the fact that I didn't have to wait on the fish to come to my bait. I would just see him and shoot him when I was ready. Bow fishing fits my personality profile better than using a pole and line and hook.

KH 2011: I wish I could tell you that I have overcome that impatient streak you have, but I still struggle with it myself. God has been real patient with me though. I'm learning, slowly, I hope.

KH 2007: What happens to me because of all the bad press? Will anyone ever let me preach at their church or teach on creation again? Quite a few of the brethren seem to have rejected me without even knowing the whole story.

KH 2011: That's classified information, but you won't believe how God is going to provide! Many have not only not rejected you, but are proud of the stand you have taken and support you now more than ever! All you can do is wait.

KH 2007: Okay. Hey, stay close in case I get more questions, would you?

KH 2011: I guess you don't know all about knee-mail yet, or you wouldn't say, "Stay close." It's always on and always instant access. I'll be here. So is everyone else.

KH 2007: Wow God! That was cool! Do you mean I can knee-mail anyone, anywhere at anytime past, present, or future?

GOD: Yes, son, and there is so much more but your CPU would explode if I told you right now.

KH: Can I knee-mail Moses while he crosses the Red Sea, Lord?

GOD: Sure, son. He's a little busy now, but he'll answer.

KH: Hey, Moses. Can you tell me what's happening?

Moses: Sure, Kent, there are about two million former slaves in a long line, all walking across the bottom of the Red Sea. The ground is rock hard and an easy slope of about five percent. The water is standing up in two walls beside us. I would guess the walls are about 600 cubits high. Pharoah is trying to get us from behind, but God keeps blocking him. God lets him stay close enough to us so that he still has hopes of catching us to destroy us.

KH: Are the people with you scared?

Moses: It is a strange mixture of emotions. I would say they are still scared, but mostly just awe struck by the events around them. I hear most of them just praising God! Nothing like this has ever happened before or even entered into the mind of man as far as I know. God is doing a totally new thing!

> *I would say these people will be changed forever by this experience. Watching God provide a way in an impossible situation against the most powerful government on earth is "cool" as you twenty-first century believers call it, beyond words or even thoughts!*

Why On Earth Did God Let This Happen... For Heaven's Sake?

KH: Please don't think I'm weird, but I've wondered something since I first heard your story as a four-year-old boy.

Moses: Go ahead, Kent. What do you want to know?

KH: Are any fish falling out of that wall of water?

Moses: Yes, Kent, thousands are.

KH: Are the people picking them up and putting them back?

Moses: Kent, these are Jews I've got here that have just been released from a 400-year prison sentence! They are keeping them for lunch later on. I saw a few children putting some back but for the most part, no.

KH: Thanks. I have always wondered about that.

Moses: You have a strange mind, Kent!

KH: I know, sorry about that. I have lots of questions for lots of people. I'll knee-mail you later, Moses.

Moses: Anytime, Kent. I'm busy right now, but one "cool" feature of knee-mail is that time is suspended for me while I answer you; so don't hesitate to ask. By the way Kent, I hear you have the most powerful government on earth after you right now. How are you doing?

KH: I'm learning (slowly) to "Stand still and see the salvation of the Lord" like you did. It's hard but I see God's power more and more. I think I will just thank Him and praise Him all of my days from now on.

Moses: Great idea, Kent! I'll see you in Heaven. We can praise God together for His deliverance.

KH: Sounds great! I can't wait.

KH: God, this is awesome! Can I ask more questions?

GOD: Later, son. Go eat lunch now.

KH: Okay, Lord. I love you!

GOD: I love you, too, son, more than your little brain can understand! One more caution, son; read Isaiah 59:1-3. Your knee-mail access can be totally blocked by your sin. Keep your lines clear, son.

KH: I'll try, Lord. I'm pretty wicked!

GOD: And I'm pretty gracious, son! Read I John 1:9!

REFLECTIONS ON JOB'S SUFFERING AND CHRISTIAN TRIALS
August 5th 2007
(based on 1 Peter 4:12 and Hebrews 12:6)

KH: Good morning, God! As I read about Job's trials, it sure seems like his ordeal took a long time. If my Bible maps are right, his three friends lived a good ways off. For them to get the message, pack for the trip, make the journey, sit there quietly for a week (Job 2:13), talk with Job for thirty-five chapters, and then marvel as You asked Your incredible questions, well.... it must have taken a long time for all this to happen. At least a few weeks and maybe even several months. During all this time, Job is suffering physically, emotionally, and mentally.

GOD: That is correct, son. It lasted a long time and Job suffered the entire time (Job 7:3).

KH: It was not just Job though, Lord. His wife suffered by watching her husband in agony. I'm sure Job had scores of other friends that were affected by this. It seems reasonable that Job's wife and ten children also would have had friends and neighbors who were deeply traumatized by these events. His circle of influence must have contained hundreds of people, Lord.

GOD: It did, son. Many hundreds knew of Job's tragedy.

KH: Plus, Job helped lots of hungry, homeless, and needy people before any of this took place (Job 29:12). Now there was no help for them from Job, so they suffered as well.

GOD: That is correct, son.

KH: I know You've been asked this many times, Lord, but why would you allow Satan to cause all this suffering?

GOD: Yes, son, I've been asked that millions of times. My response is always the same. I'm God. I do what is right.

KH: But it doesn't seem right to me, Lord. Plus millions of others down here have the same thoughts. You allow a lot of pain!

GOD: You are near sighted, son. Get better glasses.

KH: What do you mean, Lord?

GOD: How old are you, son?

KH: I'm fifty-four and a-half, Lord.

GOD: That's what percent of forever?

KH: Zero percent, Lord!

GOD: Son, the minor problems you humans face are "light" (II Corinthians 4:17) compared to the big picture. I see the big picture, son. You need new glasses.

KH: Lord, my niece broke her back and is paralyzed now. Kenny is in prison with me, Lord. He's been in a wheelchair for fourteen years now. Joni Ericson Tada has been in one for over forty years! There are many people locked up in here that are innocent but were locked up anyway because of the way the evil system works. I read Your Word and see so many people like Joseph, Naboth, Abel, Daniel, and scores of others who suffered greatly, yet had done nothing wrong. It all seems so unfair, Lord. Look at the agony my sweet wife is in!

GOD: Read Job, son. Satan does the evil, but I allow him to do it. Some people are brought very close to Me through their trials. Some get bitter. What I allow is up to Me. How they respond is up to them. Do you remember playing tennis in high school, son?

KH: Yes, Lord. I loved to play that game. I was always the number three man on the team. I never could beat the first two guys. They were real good.

GOD: Did your coach ever make you do push-ups in practice, son?

KH: Yes, Lord, all the time! He made us do hundreds of push-ups every week. It was crazy!

GOD: Did you ever have to do push-ups in a tennis match?

KH: No, Lord, I never did.

GOD: Why did he make you do them?

KH: Probably to be mean to us.

GOD: No, son. Your coach knew that push-ups use the same muscles as swinging a tennis racket. He understood what you would need to win the game and gave you exercises to get you ready for it. If you complained about the push-ups in practice because you couldn't see why he had you do them, then you needed new glasses then as well. You are "near sighted." You only look for immediate results. I see l-o-o-o-o-ng term.

KH: Am I near sighted about this prison stuff, Lord?

GOD: Yes, son, you are. It takes time before some of those guys grow to trust you. Some of the men you work with and live with don't know Me, but they are watching you like a hawk. They notice that you don't curse or steal food out of the kitchen like they do. They notice how you work hard and smile. They want the joy you have, but aren't quite ready to ask for it yet. Just be consistent, son. Keep close to Me by reading My Word. It takes time.

KH: I'm trying, Lord. I sure want to go home!

GOD: I know, son, and when I do get you out, many are going to know that I did it. Right now, wait.

KH: Okay, Lord. I'll try. But Lord, I have read scores of great books and heard sermons that have cut to my heart. I feel like I'm completely torn apart, stripped down, and not in working order now. Am I being overhauled or scrapped?

GOD: It's a complete re-build, son. You ran pretty good before, but wait until you see what I have planned! You will not believe it! For now, let me keep grinding. Hold still. I've got to plane that head. If it's not real level, it won't hold up under the high pressure where you are going to work for me.

> *All my vines that bear fruit get pruned (John 15) so they can bear more fruit. All my sons that I love go through this process (Hebrews 12:6). Even the golden furniture in my tabernacle was "beaten" into shape (Exodus 25:18,31).*
>
> *Don't think it strange that I let My children go through trials (I Peter 4:12-13). When My glory is revealed (Isaiah 40:5) (real soon, by the way!), you will be real glad I did what I did. Remember, I'm God! I do what is right (Genesis 18:25)!*

ELIJAH THE TISHBITE 'PROCLAMATION FOR NO RAIN'
August 10th 2007
(based on 1 Kings 17:1-7)

KH: Hey Elijah, how are things going?

Elijah the Tisbhite (ET): For me—real well; for the nation—not good at all. Which one do you want to hear about?

KH: Well...let's start with you. Where are you?

ET: I'm camped out by the beautiful little Brook Cherith. It flows into the Jordan River (I Kings 17:5). The water is real clear and tastes wonderful. I have a beautiful campsite.

KH: How long have you been "camping" there?

ET: About two years now.

KH: Why would you go camp by a brook for two years?

ET: Our country, Israel, has a very wicked king named Ahab. His wife, Jezebel is even more wicked. They worship the false god, Baal. The real God, the God of Israel, told me to deliver a message to Ahab and then come here and wait for my next assignment; so here I am.

KH: What message did you deliver?

ET: I told him that I represented the Lord God of Israel and that it would not rain again until I said so (I Kings 17:1).

KH: Wow! That was pretty bold! Did you know it would really work?

ET: Actually...not for sure. I'm a man just like you, Kent (James 5:17), and I suffer from doubts and fears quite frequently. I felt sure God was telling me to deliver that message to Ahab, but I sure prayed fervently every day after that (James 5:16)! I confess I had doubts, especially at first. After a few months of no rain or dew, my confidence in God grew rapidly. It wasn't like I felt I was special or that God worked for me now or anything like that. It's just that I learned that if God tells you to deliver a message, just do it and trust Him. Faith "comes" in a slow trickle sometimes rather than a quick flood. The more you read His Word, the more your faith grows (Romans 10:17).

KH: How did God speak to you? How did you know God wanted you to deliver that message? Did He actually talk out loud?

ET: No. I wish He would! That would make it so much easier! He talks to me just like He talks to everyone, through His Word. I was just a regular Jew reading my Bible when I read Deuteronomy 11 where Moses was giving his final instructions to Israel. He told them of how God would bless them if they obeyed His Word (Deuteronomy 11:7-15). He said they would always get enough rain to have great crops and live a great life. He mentions rain specifically four times. Then the fifth time He mentioned rain, it was "no rain" (Deuteronomy 11:17) because of not obeying His Word by serving other gods.

> *I know Ahab had started worshiping Baal with his wicked wife (I Kings 16:31-33); so it seemed obvious God would honor His Word and stop the rain. It was weird, but I felt a small voice in me say, "I honor my Word, Elijah. Go tell the king it won't rain."*
>
> *I was real scared; so I didn't do it right away. I kept reading and came to Deuteronomy 28 where God said it again in verse 24. The same still small voice told me to go tell the king.*
>
> *This time I had more faith; so off I went to see the king. I was still nervous, but I was also scared to not tell the king. It was obvious he wasn't reading his own Bible to seek God's face. He needed someone to tell him.*

KH: Do you consider yourself a prophet?

ET: I don't know about all that. I never went to Bible college or had anyone tell me I was "anointed" or "called." I'm just a regular guy who reads his Bible and tries to put his faith into action. Since it hasn't rained for two years, my faith has really grown! I've seen God honor His word, not my words.

KH: Did the king believe you?

ET: I don't think so. He laughed at me and said Baal would provide rain. He had a lot of his preachers tell him to ignore me. They said I was crazy. I must admit, I still had some doubts. All of his prophets have been educated lots more than me. Many have doctor's degrees and all that. They told Ahab that God really didn't say that stuff about rain "in the original language." They said they read the original "Paleo-Hebrew" and it meant something else. I don't read Paleo-Hebrew, but I know God promised to preserve His Word for all generations (Psalm 12:6-7; 119:89), so I figured my authorized version was "preserved" and I could trust it. So far, it has worked out exactly as He said.

KH: How are you eating? Do you have a job there by the brook?

ET: No job, no money, no supporters, no visitors, no friends, no credit, and no stores anywhere around here. I don't even have an orchard, vineyard, or garden. If I told you how God provides for me, you wouldn't believe me!

KH: Try me. I might.

ET: Every morning and evening a raven flies in with fresh bread and meat. Sometimes several come. I don't even know where it comes from, but it is always great and exactly enough.

KH: You are right, Elijah, that's hard to believe. The raven is one of the greediest birds on earth. They don't share anything—especially food!

ET: I know, I can't believe it myself, but it happens every day. I wish they would bring enough for a few weeks at a time, but there seems to be something about "daily bread" (Exodus 16, Matthew 4:4; 6:11; Luke 11:3). I think God likes it when we have to trust Him every day.

> *He also seems to wait until the last minute to provide as well. I read where Moses was in a hopeless situation and God opened a way across the Red Sea (Exodus 14:13-16). He did it at the last minute for Moses and He does it for me. Just when I start to feel hungry, here comes food right out of the sky! It's weird, but it works. God told me the ravens would feed me (I Kings 17:4) but I secretly still had doubts. Now, after seeing it every day for two years, it gets easier to trust God every day.*

KH: Does Ahab believe you now?

ET: I don't know for sure; since I haven't seen him or anyone else for two years. I'm sure he has noticed that it hasn't rained! I would bet his false prophets have given him some lie to believe in. God told me to hide from him (I Kings 17:3); so I did.

KH: What do you do all day?

ET: I have all my physical needs met by God every day (Philippians 4:19), so I spend time reading my Bible, praising Him and enjoying His creation. This campground is awesome! I feel like God is using this experience to completely rebuild my ox cart! As I read His Word and lots of other good books, I see more and more areas in my life that need fixed. I'm a mess!

KH: I know exactly what you mean. I feel like I'm being beaten up every day where I am too. I've read books and heard sermons that cut right to my heart. If all this cutting, grinding, soaking, and squeezing means anything, I would say God is overhauling my motor as well. I'm being blueprinted, balanced, bored, and stroked! I'll be high horsepower when He gets done!

ET: What on earth are you talking about?

KH: I'm sorry. I forgot. You don't have internal combustion engines yet.

ET: Internal what?

KH: Never mind. I'll just agree that God seems to "rebuild" us once in a while. Do you know what God is preparing you for?

ET: I have no idea. I just take one day at a time.

KH: Me too. I wish I knew what was coming and how long this rebuilding would last!

ET: So do I! I miss my family most of all! God sent me here, so here I sit. The brook is starting to dry up a little, so I have a feeling God is getting ready to do something.

KH: I read your story in the Bible and you won't believe all God is going to do with you (I Kings 17 - II Kings 2)!

ET: My story is in the Bible? I never saw it.

KH: You don't have the finished version yet. Just trust me, it's real good! God is always looking for a man that will let him be used to glorify Him (II Chronicles 16:9).

ET: But I'm just a regular guy who believes God's Word.

KH: I know, me too. I guess they are rare on earth these days.

ET: What do you mean "these days?" Who is king now where you are? What year is it?

KH: Sorry, but I can't tell you that. Plus, you probably wouldn't believe me if I told you. All I can say is, keep reading your Bible and listening to that "still small voice" (I Kings 19:12). Everything will turn out fine (Romans 8:28).

ET: I think so too. It took God forty years to rebuild the Egyptian-trained Moses into what he became. I hope your oxen can pull your internal whatever-you-called-it when God gets done with you.

KH: Ah...I'm sure the oxen will have no problem. I'll write you later.

ET: Okay. I'll be here, I think.

Why On Earth Did God Let This Happen... For Heaven's Sake?

JOSEPH'S PRISON SENTENCE
August 16th 2007

(based on Genesis 39:7-20, Isaiah 59:1-3, Matthew 21:22 and John 14:13-14)

KH: Hey Joseph! How are you doing?

Joe: Well... from man's perspective or God's?

KH: I'll take God's first.

Joe: Everything is awesome! God is the Supreme Creator of everything. He is all powerful, all knowing, in all places and fortunately—all loving and just. He has never failed to keep His promises. I'm honored to be a child in His family. Everything is great!

KH: Wow! I agree!! I can't wait to go live with Him. Now, how about from man's perspective?

Joe: Oh! It looks hopeless! I was just thrown (literally) into prison on false charges. I'm in leg irons (Psalm 105:18) in a cold, damp dungeon (Genesis 41:14) with lots of other royal prisoners. They all lost their case in court. I don't think anyone can win in Pharoah's courts! The future for me looks bad—from man's perspective.

KH: I know exactly what you mean. Hey, how much time did they give you to serve? When do you get out?

Joe: What? First of all, I don't serve time; I serve God. Secondly, all the king's sentences are for life. No one gets out of here alive unless the king himself decides it.

KH: Have you put in an appeal and explained how you were framed under false charges?

Joe: To Pharoah? Are you kidding? It would be a waste of time and money. I did put in my appeal to God. He can turn the heart of any pagan king (Proverbs 21:1).

> God watched over my father, Jacob, my grandpa Isaac, and my great-grandfather, Abraham. I trust Him to turn all this to His glory like He always does.

KH: Why did God let this happen to you?

Joe: Oh, He doesn't always tell me why, but He always does what is right.

KH: Do they let you have a Bible to read while you are there?

Joe: A what?

KH: Never mind; it hasn't all been written yet. It is God's preserved Word telling how He created the world all the way to how it will end.

Joe: I don't know about how it will end, but my dad has the preserved sacred records (Romans 3:2) that covers from the creation story (Genesis 1:1) all the way up to my uncle

Esau's family tree (Genesis 36:43; also see Creation Seminar Part Seven, Question and Answers, "Who wrote Genesis?")

KH: Well, your story is in the finished book.

Joe: My story! Why? I'm just a regular guy who has been sold into slavery and ended up in prison. This has happened to thousands of other people. Why is my story in there?

KH: I guess God likes to get the glory by fixing hopeless situations like yours. God must like the way you are trusting Him. Most of His children get angry and bitter at God when bad things happen to them.

Joe: Why? That won't do any good. Hey, you said my story is in there. My dad was writing some things when I was sold into slavery. Is that going to be part of the sacred record (II Peter 1:21)?

KH: Yes, it sure is (Genesis 37:2 - 49:32)!

Joe: Wow! Does it tell how my current situation turns out?

KH: Oh, it sure does!

Joe: Well tell me, how long will I stay in prison? Do I ever get my job back with Potiphar? Will I get to see my ten half brothers again? Do I get to see my brother Benjamin? I miss him most of all. Do I get to see my dad again? Is he even still alive?

KH: I'm sorry, Joe, but knee-mail blocks answers to future questions like that. All I can say is that God never fails or lies or abandons His children. You will be fine, Joe, real fine! Trust Him!

Joe: Okay. Hey Kent, so will you.

KH: Thanks. Hey, Joe, how long have you known the Lord?

Joe: Well, I was just a young child when my mother died giving birth to my brother Benjamin (Genesis 35:18-19); so I was basically raised by my three stepmothers. None of them really wanted me and they had lots of ways of showing their resentment as did my ten half brothers. I guess they all picked up their mothers' attitudes. I soon learned to avoid them as much as I could and spend time by myself.

> *My Dad, Jacob, saw this and started to spend lots more personal time with me. He took me with him quite often and taught me the business side of the sheep ranching industry. He also taught me all about the things of God that he had learned from his dad and grandfather.*
>
> *Dad even let me see and read the original clay tablets written by Adam, Noah, and the patriarchs. They have been passed down for centuries but perfectly preserved. They are now entrusted to Dad. I don't know who gets them next. Maybe Reuben; he is the oldest.*

> *The story of the creation and flood are proof that God is in control of the world and can handle a little guy like Pharoah or Potiphar.*

KH: So what are you doing?

Joe: I read a lot and pray. I know this is all part of my training for God's future service. My dad taught me that I'm a child of the King of Heaven. That makes me a prince! Princes must go through a lot of special training to be ready to work in the palace with the king.

> *He says that kings' children must walk, talk, and act a lot differently than regular people. It is often a very long training program that they go through. It lasts for years with refresher courses that last for life.*
>
> *My dad started training me, but my brothers were jealous and sold me into slavery (Genesis 37:27). When Potiphar bought me (Genesis 37:36), things got a lot better for a while. I was promoted to business manager of his large organization. God really blessed, and I learned a lot. More training!*
>
> *Then my master's wife tried to seduce me every day for weeks! I always said, "No" because I knew that God watches everything (Proverbs 15:3), and even this temptation was part of my training to serve in His court one day. God sends all kinds of subtle tests to prepare us.*

KH: I know. It is so cool! It's sort of like the movie, "Karate Kid." The kid thought the master had enslaved him to sand the floor, but the master was actually training the kid to fight the bully. The Karate Kid, his name was Daniel, finally got the picture.

Joe: What are you talking about? My dungeon is way beyond "cool"; it's cold. I understood that part just fine, but a "kid" is a baby goat. We don't even let them on the floor and would never even try to train them to fight a bull! They wouldn't stand a chance! Also, what is a "movie?"

KH: Oh boy! I'm sorry. That would take a long time to explain all that. Let's just say that sometimes things happen to us that we don't like or understand, but God uses it all for His glory and our good (Romans 8:28).

Joe: Now that I understand real well.

KH: I'm going through a test in my prison right now as well. Satan keeps telling me that I'm finished, done, washed up. He says he is going to destroy me, my family, and the creation ministry.

Joe: He's a liar (John 8:44). Don't listen to him. How is your prison? Do you wear leg irons like us? How long is your chain? Do you have mean rats or can you train them? How often do you get beatings from your mean guards? Do you get one small meal of rotten food scraps every day at least? The guys in here tell me that's the way it is in all the prisons they have been to. Is it the same where you are?

KH: Well....no. I'd be embarrassed to tell you about mine. It's a lot different than yours! How do you keep a good attitude in there?

Joe: I just keep looking at the bigger picture and trusting God to know what He is doing for my training. I'm pretty worried about Pharoah, though. I don't think he realizes that he just locked up one of God's children (Psalm 105:15)! I know God will step in and judge him when my training is over, so I pray that I will get a chance to tell him about God so he can repent before it is too late! Anyway, I keep a good spirit because I don't focus on the prison or the problems but the promises of God. God made a lot of promises to my family.

> *My dad actually saw God and even wrestled with Him (Genesis 32:24-30). He told me the story hundreds of times. He still limps today from that experience. I don't think his walk will ever be like it used to be.*
>
> *My grandpa Isaac also met God. He personally heard Him speak and stop his dad from killing him (Genesis 22:11). I was only thirteen when grandpa Isaac died, but he must have told me that story a thousand times. I can still repeat it word for word. He also told me about all the times his dad, that's my great-grandpa Abraham, met with God and heard Him speak (Genesis 12:1; 13:14; 14:18; 15:1-21; 17:1-22; 18:1-33; 22:1-18).*
>
> *I wish my great-great-great-great-great-great-great-great-great- grandpa Shem had lived a little longer so that I could have met him! My dad knew him. (See Longevity Chart in Seminar Notebook.) Shem told my dad all about the world before the big Flood, life on the ark, the tower of Babel (Genesis 11) and how the earth was divided in the days of Peleg (Genesis 10:25). I loved hearing those stories!*
>
> *God has a very special calling on my family. He has always provided for us even when there is a bad-looking situation like mine right now. I trust Him to fix it. Are you trusting Him to fix yours, Kent?*

KH: Well... it has been hard, but I'd say yes! I'm learning more and more each day how to lean on the everlasting arms.

Joe: I guess all we both can do is wait on the Lord (Psalm 27:14) to step in and override these politicians. I'll see you when we get to Heaven. Then you can explain why a kid would want to prepare to fight a bull on a sand floor. I really don't get any of that.

KH: Okay. I'll see ya in Heaven and explain it all. Good night for now.

Joe: Good night, Kent.

CAPTAIN OF SHIP TO ITALY WITH PASSENGERS, THE APOSTLE PAUL
August 17th 2007
(based on Acts 27:6-44)

KH: Hey Captain! I hate to bother you at this busy time, but can you talk for a minute (between verses 11 and 12)?

Captain: Sure, knee-mail suspends time; so it won't effect me at all.

KH: I understand that you own the ship that is headed to Italy.

Captain: Yes, I do. She's a beauty, isn't she!

KH: Yes, sir! It's huge too. One like this must cost a fortune!

Captain: Oh, you wouldn't believe me if I told you! This one holds nearly 300 people (27:37) plus cargo and tackling (27:19). Even though she's big, she can sail fast. I'm mighty proud of her!

KH: I heard you just decided to try to sail on for Italy. It's past good sailing time (27:9) and pretty dangerous to try now, isn't it?

Captain: I know it's the end of the season, but there is no good place to spend the winter here (27:12). I've got a great crew and a tough ship. We'll make it just fine.

KH: Isn't one of your passengers a famous preacher named Paul, and didn't he advise you not to try to sail?

Captain: Yes, he did. But why should I believe him? Let's look at the facts here. Paul is a convicted felon with a long history of legal battles. He is not a sailor or a weatherman. He has a lot of religious schooling, but it is all wrong.

> *Paul believes God guides him through life and even claims he saw the Lord in a bright light (Acts 9:3; 22:6)! Come on, Kent! This Paul guy is a certified lunatic! He claims the light knocked him off his horse. Can you believe that?*

KH: He has done some interesting miracles (Acts 13:11; 14:10; 16:18, 26; 19:11) God seems to have His hand on Paul. You may want to reconsider your decision about sailing.

Captain: No way! Paul is also part of that cult that believes God actually preserves His very words (Psalm 12:6-7 KJV). My pastor in Alexandria (Acts 27:6) says the Bible has lots of mistakes. He is a graduate of the large university in our town that is known around the world for having the largest and most complete library anywhere on earth. It is the home of the great mathematician Euclid and the 400-foot-tall Paphos lighthouse. My pastor and other scholars are working on rewriting the Bible to correct all the thousands of mistakes in it. Paul doesn't have a clue about these things. He still rejects the idea of fixing the old Bible he preaches from. I don't believe or trust his opinion on spiritual matters. We are sailing on.

KH: It seems like your mind is made up.

Captain: Yes, sir. We are packing now and leave in an hour.

KH: Just two more quick questions then. First, can you swim? Secondly, is your boat insured (27:41-44)?

Captain: Huh?

CAPTAIN OF SHIP TO ALEXANDRIA IN ACTS 28:11
August 17th 2007
(based on Acts 28:11-13)

KH: Good morning, Captain. How are things going?

Captain 2: I'm doing very well, but somewhat confused. My ship is loaded and headed for Rome, but I have a lot of inner turmoil.

KH: What seems to be causing it?

Captain 2: I just spent the last three months on the tiny island of Melita with the Apostle Paul. I listened to him preach several times a week and my faith in my home pastor is really shaken.

KH: What does Paul teach that is different?

Captain 2: Well, my pastor went to school in Alexandria at the world's most prestigious university. He is really smart and refined, but he is always correcting the Bible in his sermons. He keeps referring to "the original" Greek when I know for a fact that he and his fellow professors are rewriting the Greek text as they copy it. They leave out things that do not fit what they already believe.

> *For example, Paul teaches only believers can be baptized. My pastor likes to baptize babies and have a ceremony at the church. I think it is only for the money myself, but my pastor left out Acts 8:37 to avoid embarrassing questions about baptizing babies. They are making hundreds of changes like that.*

KH: So what are you going to do?

Captain 2: After this trip, I'm finding a new church. All the ships out of Alexandria either sink or take their passengers to Rome. I'm moving to Antioch.

KH: Great idea. All the Bibles from Alexandria either shipwreck their followers, or lead them toward Rome as well. What is the other captain going to do?

Captain 2: He still doesn't believe Paul. He is heading back to Alexandria to build another ship.

KH: Some people never learn.

DISCUSSION WITH HITLER ON EQUATING HUMANS WITH ANIMALS
August 17th 2007
(based on the Olympics hosted in Nazi Germany on August 1936)

KH: Mr. Hitler! You seem really upset! What is the problem? Why are you leaving the stadium?

Hitler: I am upset! These Olympic games are supposed to be for humans to compete against humans—not animals!

KH: I thought that was what just happened. This is the eleventh modern Olympics and I've never seen any animals involved in the competition.

Hitler: Well, you did today! Didn't you see that black, subhuman animal from America win four gold medals?

KH: Do you mean Jesse Owens?

Hitler: That's what they call him.

KH: But he's a man just like us.

Hitler: No he's not! Blacks are just animals. They have not evolved as far as other races. The world will be better off when they are gone. The only thing worse on the face of the earth is a Jew. They both must be eliminated to make more living space for the Aryan race. What race are you, Kent? You look Aryan.

KH: I'm of the human race, sir.

Hitler: No, what nationality?

KH: My ancestors came from Norway, but I'm an American.

Hitler: Norway is great! That's the birthplace of the great Aryan race! I can't believe the Americans would let an animal like Owens represent them in these games! You Americans are never going to build a great country by allowing so many subhuman varieties to breed and even interbreed with superior races. The result will be a mongrel race of inferior beings. We will never allow that in Germany.

I had hoped that these Olympic games would show the world the wisdom of our extensive eugenics program. We encourage only the fit to breed to produce a race of super human beings one day.

I'm going to complain to the Olympic games committee about their lax policy of allowing non-humans to participate. This is totally unfair.

KH: How is it decided which race is superior and what is it based on?

Hitler: It's all based on the science of evolution! Since the strongest survive and the weakest die off, we have decided to speed up the process by eliminating the inferior races of Jews and blacks. War itself will demonstrate which is the most fit race.

KH: But the Bible says that all men are of one blood (Acts 17:26).

Hitler: Oh, that Bible is outdated. Our scientists have proven man arose from apes by evolution. Only the strongest survive, and we will show the world that we are the strongest!

KH: It didn't work too well today, sir.

Hitler: That's why I'm angry!! Now, which way to the Olympic committee?

(See Creation Seminar Part Five for more information on this topic. Also see "The Pink Swastika" and "The Fourth Reich of the Rich.")

A YOUNG MAN'S DECISION - A TRUE STORY
August 19th 2007
(based on Matthew 6:33)

GOD: Good morning, son. I've been watching you sleep all night. I love you.

KH: Good morning, Lord. Thanks for protecting me and being so awesome. I can't believe that the great God of the universe would care about me. I've failed You so many times. Why do You still put up with me?

GOD: You are my child. I promised to save you and take care of you. I have great plans for you, son (Jeremiah 29:11). I love you. You seemed a little down last night as you prayed. I've got a young man I'd like you to knee-mail for me this morning. He could use someone to talk to and he may help cheer you up as well. He's sitting in his car in a parking lot. He's been crying pretty hard for a while and needs someone like you to listen to him.

KH: Sure, Lord. Where do I send it?

GOD: Pontiac, Michigan; General Motors Truck and Coach Division, Plant #6; 8:15 p.m., May 20, 1974.

KH: What should I tell him?

GOD: Just let him talk at first. You'll know what to say when he's done.

KH: OK, God.

Kent Hovind approaches the Young Man

KH: Hey, young man, it looks like you've been crying your eyes out. What's wrong?

Young Man (YM): Oh...I'll be okay. I'm just torn up inside right now. I've had some really big, life- altering decisions to make in the last year and especially in the last week. I'm only twenty-one and it's a little overwhelming to think that my decisions now will effect me for years and even forever!

KH: Yes, I know what you mean. That's the way life is, though. What's on your mind now?

YM: Well....I came up here to go to Bible college. I feel like God has called me into His service somewhere. I've been working here at this truck plant for two years now, second shift, while I went to school full-time, first shift. I got married last summer, and my sweet wife also went to school for a year. I also worked on a church bus route and taught a Sunday school class for the last two years. I graduate this Friday and I'm pretty overwhelmed with emotions right now. I'm pretty tired as well, bone tired.

KH: What is the biggest burden you carry?

YM: I guess the decision I made last night.

KH: What was it about?

YM: Last week the general foreman at work talked with me. He said they have watched me work and wanted to offer to send me to foreman school. It would mean a very secure future at General Motors. I already get paid pretty well working on the assembly line; but as foreman, I would start at about $350.00 per week plus lots of benefits and perks and bonuses. It was a dream offer for such a young man as I.

KH: So did you take it?

YM: Well....I also got an offer to work at my home church in Pekin, Illinois as assistant pastor for $100.00 per week plus a bare-bones medical plan. There are a lot of reasons to stay here. We have a real nice mobile home we are buying just two blocks from church. It is on a beautiful river with lots of ducks, swans, and fish that my wife and I feed every evening. We love our church. We have lots of friends here, and she could finish her degree.

Many people come here for Bible college and then stay on at GM. They end up as deacons or Sunday school teachers in their local churches, make real good money, and seem very happy. We could afford to start a family and buy a bigger house if I stay.

KH: So what's to decide? It looks like God is opening all the doors.

YM: Or Satan is—to distract me from my calling. I didn't come here to work at GM and build trucks. I came here to train for the ministry. Do you know where these shiny new trucks will be in thirty years?

KH: Ah...actually, yes I do. They will be rusting in a junkyard or recycled into a fence post or train track.

YM: That's right! Don't you see the real issues here? I want to invest my life in things that last forever. If I do that, God's promise in Matthew 6:33 will apply to me. God can out supply GM any day.

KH: So what did you decide?

YM: I told the general foreman, "Thanks for the offer, but I must decline." I called my home pastor and said, "Yes, I'll take the job as assistant pastor." We move next week.

KH: So why are you crying?

YM: Lots of reasons. God gave me such an amazing wife! She supports me either way. I'm crying for joy because I have her. I also have seen kids I went to school with decide this week to stay at GM. Yet they were called and trained for full-time Christian work in mission fields or ministries where the need is so great. Now the need will go unmet. That burdens me greatly as well. I don't understand why anyone would invest their life in things that will all burn, rust, or be stolen. It breaks my heart.

KH: I know exactly what you mean. Say, what's your name, young man?

YM: Kent Hovind, sir. What's yours?

KH: It's not important. You made the right choice, young man. Quit crying and start packing. You won't believe how God will supply! I have been young and now am old and have never seen God's kids begging bread (Psalm 37:25). Thanks for reminding me. It has greatly encouraged me.

YM: You are welcome. Thanks for listening.

KH: Thanks, God.

GOD: You are welcome, son. I've got your back.

GIVE ME WISDOM!
August 19th 2007
(based on Matthew 6:33)

KH: God, I don't understand. You told your children to seek after wisdom, didn't You (James 1:5)?

GOD: Yes, son. Wisdom is the principal thing. Get wisdom (Proverbs 4:7).

KH: Yet Your Word says, "In much wisdom is much grief and he that increaseth knowledge increaseth sorrow" (Ecclesiastes 1:18). I've asked You for wisdom many times, Lord.

GOD: Yes, son, so far you've asked me 181,046 times or about twelve times a day since you got saved. You do ask for wisdom a lot, son. What is the problem? I've given it to you each time.

KH: The more I learn about what is happening in the world, the more sorrow I have. Solomon was right, God. Why do you tell us to ask for wisdom (James 1:5) knowing it will bring sorrow?

GOD: I lived on earth for thirty-three and a half years as a man, son. I was a man of sorrows and acquainted with grief (Isaiah 53:3). I knew everything, even what people were thinking (Matthew 9:4; 12:15). When the rich young ruler rejected me, both he and I were sorrowful (Luke 18:23). I completely understand!

KH: But, Lord, world events are frightening! Christians are being killed and tortured by the thousands every year, Lord. The "Voice of the Martyrs" reports that more Christians have died in the last hundred years than died in the previous 1,900 years. This knowledge gives me great grief!

GOD: It is true, son. Evil men and seducers are waxing worse and worse (II Timothy 3:13) just as I foretold. These are the birth pangs, son. This age is coming to a close. I will be setting up my kingdom soon (Isaiah 65:17; II Peter 3:13; Revelation 21:1)!

Your sorrow is well founded but only short term. You need new glasses, son. You are nearsighted.

KH: But Solomon was the wisest man ever and he said wisdom causes grief.

GOD: Son, think about it. What is the theme of Ecclesiastes?

KH: It is about man's view of the world "under the sun." From man's perspective, life is vanity.

GOD: That's right, son. From man's perspective (under the sun), wisdom causes grief. I don't live under the sun. The sun won't even be needed in My new kingdom (Revelation 21:23). Solomon was right that wisdom "under the sun" brings grief, but My wisdom is from above. Go ahead and seek My wisdom, son. If your treasures are on earth, wisdom will bring sorrow; but if you set your affections on things above (Colossians 3:2), my wisdom will bring great joy.

It is true that bad times are coming soon, but I have everything under control. Evil men are planning a one-world government, but I'm laughing at the whole thing, son (Psalms 2:1-3). Keep praying for My kingdom to come (Matthew 6:10). Serve Me with gladness (Psalms 100:2). I'll fix everything one day soon.

KH: Thanks, God. I love you.

GOD: I love you too, son. More than you can know.

REUBEN - HIDDEN SIN AND FORGIVENESS
August 22nd 2007
(based on Genesis 37 and Genesis 42:1-28 as Reuben stares at his money)

KH: Hey Reuben, you look like you have seen a ghost! Are you OK?

Reuben: Uh.....no! I'm not doing well at all.

KH: What seems to be the problem?

Reuben: I just opened my sack of grain to feed my mule and found my money in it. It looks like the same money I gave the Egyptian yesterday to pay for the grain. His name was Zaphnath-paaneah (Genesis 41:45). We just call him Zaph for short. He is the second in command of the entire country right under Pharoah himself! I don't know how the money got back in my sack.

KH: Well...that's good news! You got the grain for free! What are you nervous about?

Reuben: Because Zaph will think we stole the money or the grain or both. He kept careful records of every purchase. He is going to be furious when he discovers this. He will kill us!

KH: So, just don't ever go back there to go shopping again.

Reuben: Uh...it is much more complicated than that! There is no food anywhere else because of the famine in the land, plus, Zaph kept our brother, Simeon, as a hostage until we return with our little brother, Benjamin.

KH: Why did he do that?

Reuben: Oh...it is a long, sad story.

KH: Let's hear it.

Reuben: I know that this happened because God is judging my sin. God put the money in my sack to cause all this evil. I knew this day was coming (Genesis 42:21-22).

KH: Wow, what sin did you commit?

Reuben: Lying, kidnapping, attempted murder, and withholding information from my grieving father. I helped sell my own brother into slavery and probably death! It all happened twenty-one years ago (Genesis 37:28). He was only seventeen years old. He was a good kid too! He loved God.

KH: Why did you do that? How could you sell your own brother?

Reuben: I come from a very dysfunctional family and it would be easy to blame my childhood, but since I'm the oldest and knew better, it is all largely my fault.

KH: Tell me about your childhood.

Reuben: My dad, Jacob, deceived his own father and stole his brother's birthright and blessing (Genesis 27). That would be my Uncle Esau. He had to run away from his furious brother so he came to Haran and got a job working for my grandpa Laban (Genesis 28:10). Grandpa Laban tricked Dad into marrying my mom when he really wanted to marry her younger sister, my aunt Rachel (Genesis 29:25). Mom knew she wasn't really pretty and Dad didn't really love her. Their marriage was pretty shaky from the start.

When I was born, Mom tried to use me to get Dad's attention (Genesis 29:32). I didn't feel much love either. It was more like I was just a pawn in some game they were playing. My mom's sister was real pretty but she was a liar and a thief (Genesis 31:34) just like Dad.

Both sisters were jealous of each other and talked Dad into marrying their servant girls to have even more children. It was a real mess! I had three stepmothers who were all jealous of each other, all fighting for Dad's attention; and all resented me. I also had five brothers and five half brothers and one sister. Later I got another half brother.

KH: Wow! What a messed up family! That's a bad way to grow up.

Reuben: Yes, it was! Dad was too busy with family feuds to really spend much time teaching us things. He was often scheming up ways to trick people and get rich quick. He even cheated my Grandpa Laban out of his sheep and goats (Genesis 30:32-43).

Dad knew Grandpa would be mad; so he packed us all up and left without letting us even say goodbye to Grandpa (Genesis 31:17). That hurt bad, too! Dad tried to be all holy about stealing the flocks. He said God had given them to him (Genesis 31:8-9).

Ha! We boys all knew what really happened. We helped Dad artificially inseminate the flocks (Genesis 30:37-39). That's one thing Dad taught us a lot about—mating! I think we all knew way too much way too soon! I won't do that with my kids. It was real hard to keep a clean heart and mind around our house. There seemed to be only one thing on everyone's mind.

My mom even taught me about aphrodisiacs! I found some mandrakes (Genesis 30:14) one time and knew what they were for and that Mom would want them. How is a teenage boy supposed to keep a clean mind growing up with a mom and dad like that (Psalm 119:9-11). Our house was filled with lustful thoughts and talk all the time. I even committed adultery with one of my stepmoms (Genesis 35:22). Dad knew about it but didn't do anything. He never taught me to admit my sin and take responsibility for my actions.

KH: Sounds like a lot of families in my town. Kids are raised with a steady stream of immorality in their living room right on the TV. Then parents wonder why their kids go bad.

Reuben: On a what? What's a TV?

KH: Never mind. That would take a while to explain! Why didn't your dad do anything?

Reuben: I don't know. I wish he would have been more consistent as a parent. It was almost as if he were two different people. Sometimes all he lived for was the flesh and other times he was real close to God. He even has two names: Jacob and Israel. He is definitely a double-minded man (James 1:8).

KH: What does all this have to do with the money in the sack?

Reuben: I'm just giving you the background on why I'm unstable (Genesis 49:4). It's not really an excuse, but I sure didn't have any good role models in the house except Joseph. He was the only one of us boys who really seemed to want to stay pure and serve God. We pretty much hated him for it.

KH: So do you recommend that men have multiple wives or girlfirends?

Reuben: No way! It causes lots of problems in the family! Anyway, when Dad made Joseph the coat of many colors, the brothers really got mad. They plotted to kill him but I talked them out of that. We just threw him in a pit (Genesis 37:18-24). I left to take care of the sheep and when I came back, I found out my brothers had sold him to be a slave (Genesis 37:29-30)! That's when we decided to dip his coat in blood and give it to Dad (Genesis 37:31-32). We didn't technically lie to Dad. We just showed him the bloody coat and let him think Joseph had been torn up by animals.

KH: Did it bother you?

Reuben: Real bad. Sometimes withholding truth is just like lying. It has bothered me every day and night for twenty-one years! When Dad saw the coat, he cried uncontrollably for weeks (Genesis 38:34) and still has bad days even now. I have not been able to have an open, honest loving relationship with my dad for twenty-one years now. My secret sin affects my relations with my brothers and even my wife and children. I always feel like I'm hiding something because I am! The burden I carry is horrible! Every time anything bad happens, even if I just break a fingernail, I am reminded of my sin. It is awful to live this way (1 Kings 17:18)!

I've thought of that day thousands of times! I want so badly to get this off my conscience. I'm just too unstable, I guess (Genesis 49:4). I find it hard to talk with Dad. We all knew he had lied and tricked both his dad and his brother (Genesis 27). We were also pretty mad when our only sister was defiled and Dad did nothing about it (Genesis 34:5)!

I know it's no excuse for me, but our family has a long history of lies, lust, and greed. Now, it is all catching up with us (Genesis 42:21; Numbers 32:23). If this famine continues, we will all starve. Zaph told us not to come back without our little brother, Benjamin (Genesis

42:20). There is no way Dad will ever let Ben go with us all the way to Egypt. God is definitely judging us. The way of the transgressor is so hard (Genesis 4:13; Proverbs 13:15). It would have been so much better to just live for God and do right (Proverbs 28:13)!

KH: Wow! Now I see why the money in the sack does not make you happy. You have a real mess on your hands!

Reuben: I know! I dread facing Dad. I dread facing Zaph again and I really dread facing God! I've pretty well messed up my life and my kids' lives. I don't see any way out of this problem.

KH: Well...God is merciful to those who confess their sins and forsake them (I John 1:9). He can even use our sin, selfishness, stupidity and stubborness for His glory and for our good. I was pretty stupid one time as a seventeen-year-old. I tapped out the head bolts on my Volkswagon to put in Heli-coils and didn't take time to change the oil afterwards. I blew the engine on a date that night, but that's how I ended up with my gorgeous wife!

Reuben: Huh? What's a head bolt and why do you tap on them? How many oxen are needed to pull a "volks" or whatever kind of wagon it was you had? I don't get anything you are talking about!

KH: Oh, boy! That would take a real long time to explain, but the point is, God used my mistake for His glory. He will do the same with you if you confess your sin. Come clean, Reuben! God still loves you and can even fix this horrible mess you've made.

Reuben: There is no way even God can fix this one. I've messed it up too bad.

KH: Go home and pray about it. Don't let your dad suffer anymore. Tell him the truth.

Reuben: I'll pray about it, but I don't think God listens to me or even wants me.

KH: Oh, He listens and wants you, but it starts with admitting your sin to Him and then following His steps to make it right with the people you've harmed.

Reuben: How could I ever fix the wrong I've done to my brother, Joseph? He's got to be dead by now!

KH: Didn't Joseph try to keep a pure heart and serve God?

Reuben: Yes, he was not perfect, but he did trust God and tried to do right. But it didn't do any good. Look what happened to him! He died!

KH: Actually, I know how God will fix that one, too, but I can't tell you.

Reuben: Why not?

KH: First, knee-mail blocks stuff about the future most of the time; and second, you wouldn't believe me if I told you how it all turns out.

Reuben: How do you know this stuff?

KH: God keeps His Word. He promised to bless your father, Jacob, your grandfather, Isaac, and your great-grandfather, Abraham. God never lies. Plus, I read the end of your story in God's Word (Revelation 7:5). You'll be fine (Deuteronomy 33:1-6)!

Reuben: My story is in God's Word?

KH: Oh, yes! Many times.

Reuben: So, God will straighten this terrible mess out? How?

KH: I can't tell you how, but get ready to shout praises to God when He does. You know you will eventually have to confess your sin. Why not do it now?

Reuben: I can't. Maybe next year.

KH: Yes, maybe next year. I hate to see you hide this sin and waste another year of your life, but it's your decision. I will knee-mail you later on. Enjoy your trip home.

PRESSURE
August 26th 2007
(based on Matthew 6:33)

GOD: Hey, son, it's 3:30 a.m. Why aren't you sleeping?

KH: I was sleeping fine, Lord, but I woke up with a lot on my mind. I've been under a lot of *pressure* lately, Lord. So has my wife, my family, and my ministry. This year-long legal battle has produced a lot of pressure in many ways, especially financially. I also feel a deep yearning to be with my family and back out spreading Your Gospel. I guess it all woke me up.

GOD: Didn't you go to bed asking Me to handle all those things?

KH: Yes, Lord, I did.

GOD: Then why are you still carrying all that load, son? Don't you trust me (I Peter 5:7)?

KH: I guess not like I should, Lord. I'm sorry.

GOD: Well son, let me explain a few things to you about pressure (II Corinthians 1:8). First, pressure is good. I created it. It is required to get the juice from the fruit, the oil from the olive and the fragrance from the flower. Without pressure, the rivers would not flow nor the water in your plumbing. It keeps the electrons flowing in the wires to light the room and turn the motor in the AC unit, which then supplies pressure to compress the Freon and force the air to circulate to cool the building.

Your diaphragm pulls down on your lungs as you breathe and air pressure all around you forces air into your lungs to keep you alive. It is pressure that gets the oxygen from your lungs into the blood stream which is moved around your body by more pressure supplied by your heart, arteries, and capillaries.

It is pressure that keeps all your cells inflated and makes your eyeballs round so you can see to read My Word and enjoy My world.

Pressure keeps the ink flowing out of the pen you hold and press against the paper which is made of fibers pressed into sheets and cut by pressure.

Pressure keeps strings tight in a piano so that when they are struck (more pressure), they vibrate and exert pressure on the air around them which makes your eardrum move, and you can hear the music.

Pressure lets you chew your food and turn your head to see the air pressure, called wind, rustle the leaves on the trees, that exist because of root pressure pushing water up to make them grow and push water and nutrients into the fruit, for you to chew or squeeze with more pressure.

Pressure also forces various materials into more usable shapes. Wasn't that pen you are holding formed and filled using pressure? Weren't the parts of that table you are sitting at and the parts of the building you are in all formed by pressure? Isn't the building you are in held in place by pressure?

KH: Yes, Lord. It is all true.

GOD: *Pressure* also keeps things moving, son. Does your pen move by itself?

KH: No, Lord. I provide the pressure. By itself, it would do nothing.

GOD: And even when you move it, the results are hard to read. You need to work on your handwriting, son.

KH: I know, Lord. Sorry about that.

GOD: Every time you walk you put *pressure* on the floor. Where would you be without the relentless pressure of gravity?

KH: I'd be lost in space, Lord.

GOD: Yes you would, son. *Pressure* is good. I created it. Secondly son, don't you humans have thousands of ways of using *pressure*? Don't you have thousands of instruments and expensive gauges to monitor and regulate the *pressure* on millions of things you do down there?

KH: Yes, Lord, we do.

GOD: If you didn't keep the *pressure* just right your pipes would explode, your electrical wires would all melt, and your tires would go flat. Don't you think I'm smart enough to monitor the *pressure* I allow on My children (Mark 1:35; I Corinthians 10:13; I Peter 5:7)?

KH: Yes, Lord, You are.

GOD: Aren't you careful to use just the right *pressure* on the steering wheel, the gas, and the brakes as you drive?

KH: I try, Lord.

GOD: That's a good point, son. You, your second son, and your daughter all need to use a little less *pressure* on the gas pedal!

KH: Oh, Lord, you are right. I'll tell them.

GOD: Don't you humans use *pressure* to squeeze lots of things into a desired shape, to be more useful to yourselves?

KH: Yes, Lord. Millions of things from pancakes to space shuttles require *pressure* to produce.

GOD: Don't you think that I know how much *pressure* to use to get you into the desired shape (Romans 8:29)?

KH: Yes, Lord, You know.

GOD: I'm monitoring all the gauges, son. I know exactly how much *pressure* you are under, how much you can stand, and how much is needed to get you into the desired shape. Everything is under control. Trust me.

KH: I'm trying, Lord. It just hurts, that's all.

GOD: *Pressure* often hurts, son, but it is required to get the job done. You have circuit breakers to make sure your wires don't get too much *pressure* and pop off valves to be sure your water heater doesn't explode. I've got ways to get excess *pressure* off of you, son. Didn't the judge grant the Motion for Release Pending Appeal to keep your wife from going to prison August 31st?

KH: Yes, Lord, she did.

GOD: Didn't that take a lot of *pressure* off all of you?

KH: Yes, Lord, it sure did. Thanks!

GOD: That's just the beginning, son. Lots of items you use were formed under pressure, but once the item is formed, the pressure can be taken off. I'm forming you, son (Genesis 2:7; Proverbs 26:10; Isaiah 43:7; 44:2; Galatians 4:19). I'll relieve the *pressure* when it's time.

KH: I know, Lord, I feel the *pressure*. Thanks for working with me.

GOD: It's my pleasure, son. I work with all my children like this (Romans 8:29-30; 12:1-2; Philippians 1:6). I can squeeze a lot into a little. You should see the power I squeezed into uranium and plutonium atoms! I know precisely how much *pressure* to use to make a seam of coal, a pool of oil, and a diamond.

I know exactly what *pressure* you need to get you where I want you. Hold still, son. Patience means to bear up under *pressure*. Be patient, son. Trust me.

KH: I'm trying, but I am not good at all with patience!

GOD: Thirdly, son, if the *pressure* is too great, I will carry the excess load (Matthew 11:29-30). I will never give you more than you can bear (I Corinthians 10:13). The pipes in my house don't burst and my tires never go flat. I don't get tired or surprised.

KH: God, are you squeezing me to get something out of me, get something into me, or get me in a more usable shape?

GOD: All three and more, son. If I told you everything I was doing, your little brain would not be able to handle it all.

I've gotten some prayers and writings from you that you didn't have time for in the free world. I've had you read things, watch things, hear things, and experience things that have changed you forever. I can squeeze things into you and out of you at the same time.

I'm getting some oil, fragrance, and juice out of you that is helping nourish, refresh, and bless some of your brothers and sisters in Christ. I'm also using you to convict and convert others who were not My children until they saw you get squeezed like this.

I can squeeze all positive protons together in atoms; then squeeze the atoms into metal to make a trumpet (I Corinthians 15:52; I Thessalonians 4:16; Revelation 1:10) which I will very soon squeeze air through to call My children home! I can put the needed *pressure* in the right spots to cause every knee to bow and every tongue to confess that Jesus Christ is Lord to My glory (Isaiah 45:23; Romans 14:11).

I can supply the *pressure* to open the prison doors (Acts 5:19; 12:7; 16:26) and cause even the heathen to praise My name. I'm in charge. I'm God!

KH: I know, God, I'm sorry to doubt. Sometimes I just forget.

GOD: It's all under My control. Go to sleep. When you get up, relax, enjoy My Word and My world. Get a tan, read a book, and let's talk some more. Forget the *pressure*, son. I'll take it from here. I've got your back.

LUTHER BRIDGERS - A SONG BORN IN TRAGEDY
August 26th 2007

GOD: Hey, son, we had good fellowship today, didn't we?

KH: Yes, Lord! You are awesome! This book, Finding Favor with the King by Tommy Tenney is just what I needed. Thanks for letting me have it, Lord. I feel like I've been screaming outside the gates. I want to be right next to You. Please cover me with Your righteousness so we can stay close.

GOD: You keep your walk, hands, and mind clean, son (Psalm 24:4). Always stop at the altar first before you come close. I only accept clean people into My presence (Leviticus 16:1-4).

KH: Thanks for being willing to clean me over and over again, Lord.

GOD: I never tire of it, son. I've got a knee-mail I'd like you to write. You look a little down this evening.

KH: Sure, Lord, to whom?

GOD: Send it to Luther Bridgers in 1910. He's crying pretty hard right now, but you will be encouraged just by talking with him.

KH: Ok, Lord.

Kent Hovind approaches Mr. Luther Bridgers

KH: Excuse me, Mr. Bridgers, I can't help but see you are deeply hurt over something. Can I help you?

Luther Bridgers (LB): Oh, thanks for asking. Just pray for me. I'm filled with mixed emotions right now after this great tragedy.

KH: What happened?

LB: I've been preaching for nine years now. I was out of town preaching a revival meeting; so my wife and three sons went to her parents' house in Kentucky for a visit. The house caught fire during the night. Her parents got out alive, but my wife and three boys all died in the fire.

KH: Wow, that is terrible! I'm so sorry to hear about it. Is there anything I can do?

LB: Just pray. God has come so close to me during this tragedy. He is even giving me a song I think. The funeral is tomorrow. All I could pray at first was just Jesus, Jesus, Jesus. Just calling His name was a comfort. He understands my grief and fills my heart. He keeps me singing during the good and the bad of life.

KH: Can I hear what you have written so far?

LB: I'm not a great musician and it's not done yet, but so far it goes,

> "There's within my heart a melody, Jesus whispers sweet and low; Fear not I am with thee, peace be still; In all of life's ebb and flow. Jesus, Jesus, Jesus, Sweetest name I know. Fills my every longing; Keeps me singing as I go."

KH: I love it! He can keep us singing even when tragedy strikes.

LB: I know. He has for me. Do you think the song will ever help anyone else?

KH: You wouldn't believe me if I told you how God is going to use this tragedy for HIS glory.

LB: Really? I'm so glad. I just want to be used of God to bring people to Heaven.

KH: You will, Luther. You will. I'll pray for you. Finish your song. I have a feeling God will use it. It sure blessed me!

LB: Thanks for your encouragement, Kent. I'll see you in Heaven.

KH: God, I'm sorry for griping about my little trials down here. If Luther Bridgers can sing after losing his wife and three sons in a fire while he was preaching, I guess I can sing in prison, can't I?

GOD: Yes, son, you can. I know all about your situation. I'm in control. I'm God. Go sing, son. I've got your back.

WIDOW WOMAN
August 27th 2007

GOD: Hey son, you still seem to be struggling with trusting me to supply.

KH: I'm sorry, Lord, you are right. I do still struggle. Between the legal costs and the bad publicity, our ministry finances are pretty bad. I told you I would preach as long as you supplied.

GOD: Have I supplied so far?

KH: Yes, Lord, You have been faithful for eighteen years now supplying for the ministry.

GOD: I'd like you to knee-mail someone for me. It will help you.

KH: Sure, Lord. Where do I send it?

GOD: There is a widow woman who has your same doubts right between II Kings 4:5 and 6. Talk to her.

KH: OK, Lord.

Kent Hovind approaches the Widow Woman

KH: Excuse me Ma'am. Can I ask what on earth you are doing?

Widow Woman (WW): Yes. My sons and I have borrowed lots of pots, pans, bowls, and pitchers from our neighbors.

KH: I see that! The house is pretty full of containers. What for?

WW: I don't know for sure. My preacher Elisha told me to do it so I did. He loves God and always has good advise.

KH: How long have you known Elisha?

WW: Several years now. My husband and I came down here for my husband to go to Bible college (II Kings 4:1; II Kings 2:3;6:1; I Samuel 10:10;19:20). Elisha is the teacher. He is a real good one, too. He studied under the great Elijah himself (I Kings 19:19 - II Kings 2:15).

KH: How does your husband like the school?

WW: Well....he loved it, but he died last year. Now my two sons and I are way behind on rent and the camel payment, too. The current laws allow the creditors to sell my sons into slavery to pay the bills. We have been praying a lot! We're desperate!

KH: I'm so sorry to hear about your husband and the great financial stress you have. How do the pots and pans fit in?

WW: I went to Elisha with my prayer request (II Kings 4:1), and he said, "Go borrow vessels, not a few" (II Kings 4:3). So I did. I agree that it seems a little crazy, but God works in unusual ways sometimes.

KH: What is Elisha going to do?

WW: I don't know, but I trust God to provide. If He doesn't come through by noon tomorrow, my boys get sold. Why does God always wait until the last minute?

KH: I don't know. Maybe He wants to get all the glory. He sure deserves it!

WW: That must be it. I struggle with doubts and depression since my husband died. I know I should be a stronger believer. It's just hard.

KH: I know, I struggle as well. I read your story, though. Everything will be fine.

WW: Where did you read my story?

KH: Ah....it's pretty famous, but I can't tell you right now. Just do what Elisha says. He has a direct link to God.

WW: OK. He's calling me now. We'll talk later.

KH: I look forward to it!

Kent Hovind leaves the Widow Woman

KH: God, You are right, as usual. I know you supplied for her because I have hindsight. You will take care of me, too, won't You?

GOD: Of course, son. Haven't I always?

KH: Yes, Lord. You used that cruise to fill the emptiness in lots of other vessels.

GOD: Yes, Son, I did.

KH: Will you use me again, to tell them about You so that You can fill the void in people's lives?

GOD: Yes, Son. Go take a shower, Son, you stink. Then, take a twenty-minute nap. I've got your back.

ESSAY ON JOHN BUNYAN'S TRIAL
August 30th 2007

John Bunyan wrote Pilgrim's Progress while in Bedford Jail. He was jailed for refusing to take a license to preach. Here is the transcript of his trial. Some do not understand why Daniel prayed in Daniel 6:10, why Shadrach stood in Daniel 3:13, why Moses refused Pharoah's "generous" offer in Exodus 8:25,28; 10:11; 10:24, or why Samuel insisted on complete obedience in I Samuel 15:10-33. They don't comprehend why the midwives ignored Pharoah in Exodus 1:17 or why the disciples endured being beaten, threatened, jailed, or killed in fifty-three accounts in Acts alone instead of conforming to nonbiblical mandates.

These same people will never understand why John Bunyan spent fourteen years in jail rather than take a license. I don't think I can explain it to them. Read the following transcript from his trial and weep for America.

When the authorities say, "Take this mark or you can't buy or sell," I'll starve (Revelation 13:16-17; 14:9-11; 16:1-2). What will you do?

God has your back,
Kent

The great Baptist preacher and author John Bunyan (1628-1688) was arrested and imprisoned under Charles II for preaching without a license and for failure to attend the Anglican church. The following is an actual court record of Bunyan's trial. It was recently discovered among the papers of Thomas Breedlove.

Judge Wingate: This court would remind you, sir, that we are not here to debate the merits of the law. We are here to determine if you are, in fact, guilty of violating it.

Bunyan: Perhaps, M'lord, that is why you are here, but it is most certainly not why I am here. I am here because you compel me to be here. All I ask is to be left alone to preach and to teach as God directs me. As, however, I must be here, I cannot fail to use these circumstances as an opportunity to speak against what I know to be an unjust and odious edict.

Judge Wingate: Let me understand you. You are arguing that every man has a right, given him by Almighty God, to seek the Deity in his own way, even if he chooses to seek his Deity without benefit of the English Church?

Bunyan: This is precisely what I am arguing, M'lord. Or without benefit of any church.

Judge Wingate: Do you know what you are saying? What of Papists and Quakers? What of pagan Mohammedans? Have these the right to seek God in their own misguided way?

Bunyan: Even these, M'lord.

Judge Wingate: Yet, you affirm a God-given right to hold any alien religious doctrine that appeals to the warped minds of men?

Bunyan: I do, M'lord.

Judge Wingate: I find your views impossible of belief. And what of those who, if left to their own devices, would have no interest in things heavenly? Have they the right to be allowed to continue unmolested in their error?

Bunyan: It is my fervent belief that they do, M'lord.

Judge Wingate: And on what basis, might I ask, can you make such a rash affirmation?

Bunyan: On the basis, M'lord, that a man's religious views—or lack of them—are matters between his conscience and his God and are not the business of the Crown, the Parliament, or even with all due respect, M'lord, of the court.

However much I may be in disagreement with another man's sincerely held religious beliefs, neither I nor any other may disallow his right to hold those beliefs. No man's rights in these affairs are secure if every other man's rights are not equally secure.

Judge Wingate: It is obvious, sir, that you are a victim of deranged thinking. If my ears deceive me not, I must infer from your words that you believe the State to have no interest in the religious life of its subjects.

Bunyan: The State, M'lord, may have an interest in anything in which it wishes to have an interest. But the State has no right whatever to interfere in the religious life of its citizens.

Judge Wingate: You are a tinker by trade, are you not, Mr. Bunyan?

Bunyan: That is correct, M'lord.

Judge Wingate: Would you mind apprising this Court of the extent of your formal schooling?

Bunyan: Not at all, M'lord. Able am I to read and write, and that with difficulty.

Judge Wingate: I surmised as much. I think I perceive why you are unable to appreciate the disaster that would accompany your views should ever they hold sway in our society. I myself—and I say this in all modesty—am not inconsiderably trained in the historian's discipline. If you were half so well-versed yourself, you would instantly recognize the fatal flaw in your reasoning. Throughout history, virtually every significant human tragedy has come about as a result of divergent religious views. Nation against nation. Brother against brother. War. Destruction. Devastation time and again. And why? I shall tell you why, sir. It is because men cannot agree on which God to worship, and how to worship Him.

Now, after a long and arduous struggle, we have succeeded in conformity in the religious beliefs of all Englishmen. All our problems will be resolved when everyone finally agrees to accommodate himself and adopt the same orthodoxy of religious opinion. No more religious wars. No more divisive doctrinal disputes! Think of it, Mr. Bunyan! Does this not portend a society of which any man would be proud and happy to be a part?

Bunyan: To a degree, M'lord, it admittedly does. But only if everyone can be convicted by virtue of reasoning alone to adopt identical views of God. The society that you describe is an appealing one, but I fear the cost is far too high. It would necessitate that honest men repudiate convictions honestly held.

Judge Wingate: You are, Mr. Bunyan, a strong-willed and opinionated man. Yet this Court finds it fascinating to speak with you, and wishes time permitted further discussion of our respective philosophies. But alas, time is passing swiftly, and other cases await our attention. Let us move, then, to the matter before us, shall we? The evidence I hold in my hand—even apart from your own admission of guilt—is sufficient to convict you, and the Court is within its rights to have you committed to prison for a considerably long time. I do not wish to send you to prison, Mr. Bunyan. I am aware of the poverty of your family, and I believe you have a little daughter who, unfortunately, was born blind. Is this not so?

Bunyan: It is, M'lord.

Judge Wingate: Very well. The decision of the Court is this: In as much as the accused has confessed his guilt, we shall follow a merciful and compassionate course of action. We shall release him on the condition that he swear solemnly to discontinue the convening of religious meetings, and that he affix his signature to such an oath prior to quitting the Courtroom. That will be all, Mr. Bunyan. I hope not to see you here again. May we hear the next case?

Bunyan: M'lord, if I may have another moment of the Court's time?

Judge Wingate: Yes, but you must be quick about it. We have other matters to attend to. What is it?

Bunyan: I cannot do what you ask of me, M'lord. I cannot place my signature upon any document in which I promise henceforth not to preach. My calling to preach the Gospel is from God, and He alone can make me discontinue what He has appointed me to do. As I have had no word from Him to that effect, I must continue to preach, and I shall continue to preach.

Judge Wingate: Mr. Bunyan, you are trying the patience of this Court!

Bunyan: That is not my intention, M'lord.

Judge Wingate: I warn you, sir, the Court has gone the second mile to be lenient with you, out of concern for your family's difficult straits. Truth to tell, it would appear that the Court's concern for your family far exceeds your own. Do you wish to go to prison?

Bunyan: No, M'lord. Few things there are that I would wish less.

Judge Wingate: Very well, then, Mr. Bunyan. This Court will make one further attempt in good faith to accommodate what appears to be strongly held convictions on your part.

In his compassion and beneficence, our Savereign, Charles II, has made provision for dissenting preachers to hold some limited meetings. All that is required is that such ministers procure licenses authorizing them to convene these gatherings. The Court will not require you to sign any documents, but will require only your verbal commitment to proceed through proper channels to obtain licenses. You will not find the procedure burdensome, and even you, Mr. Bunyan, must surely grant the legitimacy of the State's interest in ensuring that any fool with a Bible does not simply gather a group of people together and begin to preach to them. Imagine the implications were that to happen! Can you comply with this condition, Mr. Bunyan?

Before you answer, mark you this: should you refuse, the Court will have no alternative but to sentence you to a prison term. Think, sir, of your poor wife. Think of your children, and particularly of your pitiful, sightless little girl. Think of your flock, who can hear you to their hearts' content when you have secured your licenses. Think of these things, and give us your answer, sir!

Bunyan: M'lord, I appreciate the Court's efforts to be—as you have put it—accommodating. But again, I must refuse your terms. I must repeat that it is God who constrains me to preach, and no man or company of men may grant or deny me leave to preach. These licenses of which you speak, M'lord, are symbols not of a right, but of a privilege. Implied therein is the principle that a mere man can extend or withhold them according to his whim. I speak not of privileges, but of rights. Privileges granted by men may be denied by men. Rights are granted by God, and can be legitimately denied by no man. I must therefore, refuse to comply.

Judge Wingate: Very well, Mr. Bunyan. Since you persist in your intractability, and since you reject this Court's honest effort at compromise, you leave no choice but to commit you to Bedford jail for a period of six years. If you manage to survive, I should think that your experience will correct your thinking. If you fail to survive, that will be unfortunate. In any event, I strongly suspect that we have heard the last we shall ever hear from Mr. John Bunyan. Now, may we hear the next case.

PS Today many preachers will quote or read the Pilgrims Progress, but very few will ever mention the fact that Pastor John Bunyan spent fourteen years in prison because he refused to accept the 501(c)(3) of his day. He knew that to be licensed by the State would be to acknowledge the State and not Christ, as the Head of the Church (Matthew 6:24-34).

GOD AND THE YOUNG BOY - CATERPILLAR POWER PARADE
August 30th 2007

GOD: Hey, Son, good morning! I love you!

KH: Good morning, Lord. I love you, too. I'm sure ready to get back out preaching for you, Lord. Can I go home now?

GOD: Do you think I need you out preaching for Me?

KH: No, Lord. I know You don't need me, but I need to be used. Even the dogs get the crumbs, you know (Mark 7:28).

GOD: I know, Son. Good answer. I'll send you back out soon. I want you to knee-mail a very excited seven-year-old for Me.

KH: Sure, Lord. When and where?

GOD: Peoria, Illinois; Caterpillar Tractor Company Proving Grounds in Marquette Heights; just after the Power Parade in 1960

KH: Hey there, Son. You look excited! Where have you been?

Young Boy (YB): I'm very excited! I just watched the Power Parade. My daddy works at Caterpillar Tractor Company where they make all kinds of big machines to move dirt and rocks. Every ten years, they have a public demonstration of their newest machines. It was s-o-o-o-o-o cool!

KH: Tell me about it.

YB: The show started when the man said, "Welcome to the Power Parade." Just then a clown walked out pushing a wheelbarrow with a shovel in it. The announcer asked the clown what he was doing and the clown used hand signals to tell him he was going to dig a basement for a house.

The announcer asked him how big it was going to be, and the clown, with his big floppy feet, walked off a rectangle twenty-four feet by forty feet and put a stake at each corner. The clown said it would be seven feet deep.

KH: Did he really dig a hole that big with a shovel?

YB: Well...he started digging at the beginning of the show and dug for the whole two hours, but he didn't get a very big hole. It was more like the size of a grave.

While he was digging the announcer said, "Well, folks, we'll let our clown friend dig it the old-fashioned way while we show you how we do it at Caterpillar."

Just then, a small D1 bulldozer came over the hill and started digging a basement the same size near the clown's basement. It took the D1 two hours, but he did it.

KH: Is that all you did was watch them dig holes?

YB: Oh, no! While they were racing to see who could dig their basement the fastest, lots of other machines came over the hill to show what they could do. They had six backhoes doing a square dance. It was s-o-o-o-o-o cool! They all had their buckets up in the air almost touching in the middle of the circle while the announcer said, "Swing your partner round and round." They spun around and drove around in circles at the same time. It was just like they were dancing!

Every once in a while, the clown would run over to check the size of the hole the D1 was making. Then he would run back to his hole and dig faster. It was so funny. The D1 was beating him really badly, but they both kept working for the whole show.

KH: What else did you see?

YB: They showed us all kinds of machines that Caterpillar makes. Some are for scraping to make roads. They had several sizes of those. They also had some that the belly dropped down to scoop up dirt. If they got stuck, a bulldozer would come push them. It was so loud.

I really love my dad! I'm so glad he works for a company that makes powerful machines like this. My dad is s-o-o-o-o-o smart!

KH: What was your favorite part of the show?

YB: Oh, the last part! When the D1 finished digging his basement, he had piled up a huge mountain of dirt. Then he drove over to the front of the crowd and raised and lowered his blade like he was waving to us. We all clapped and cheered. The clown gave up digging and sat down in his wheelbarrow by his tiny hole and frowned.

Right then, we heard this really loud roar and felt the bleachers shake as the new D9 bulldozer came over the hill! It was huge! It drove over to where the D1 had dug the big hole for the basement and pushed all the dirt back in the hole in one push! I mean the hole was filled back in, in five seconds!

My dad told me the new D9 was big, but I couldn't believe it! Then the D9 dug a new basement in two minutes! The clown just fell over and acted like he fainted. We laughed and cheered. It was s-o-o-o-o-o cool!

KH: Wow! That must have really made an impression on you, young man. Say, what's your name?

YB: I'm Kent, sir. My dad is Bob Hovind. I've got to go now. My dad knows some of the guys that drove the machines in the show. He's going to let me meet them and shake hands. Good bye!

KH: Good bye, Kent. I'm glad you enjoyed the Power Parade!

KH: Thanks, God. I think I see it now. I'm the D1 and You are the D9, right?

GOD: No, Son. You are the ant under the clown's wheelbarrow and I'm the D1. The I is for Infinite! I'm moving the entire earth right now at sixty-six thousand miles per hour and not even breaking a sweat. Not to mention the other planets and stars.

I don't need you to help, Son, but I love you and enjoy watching you work. Just don't get the idea that you are real important or accomplishing a lot for Me, OK?

KH: OK, Lord. I like watching ants work as well, Lord. Plus, I really like working for a smart Dad like You Who can create the universe just by speaking! I love you, Daddy!

GOD: I love you, too, Son. I'll send you back out soon. I've got your back.

MOTIVES FOR READING GOD'S WORD
September 1st 2007

GOD: Good morning, son.

KH: Good morning, Lord.

GOD: I see you are reading My Word.

KH: Yes, Lord.

GOD: Why?

KH: Why am I reading Your Word?

GOD: Yes, son, why are you reading it? Examine your heart. Are you reading because you feel obligated? What's your motive?

KH: I guess I never thought about it, Lord. There are lots of reasons to read it.

GOD: Yes, son, there are lots of reasons people read My Word. Some read it because of habit. Habits are good, son, and I want all My children to get good habits and avoid bad habits, but habit alone is not a good reason to read My Word.

Some only read it to get a message to preach to others. Some read it to salve their conscience. It makes them feel that they have done their daily duty to Me. Some read it so that they can impress others with their Bible knowledge; some so they can win a debate; and others so they can brag and say, "I have read my Bible every day for X number of years. I have read it cover to cover X times (Luke 18:11-12)!" Some read their "chapter a day to keep the devil away." Some think reading My Word obligates Me to protect them or provide special blessings to them. Thus, thinking that My Word is a magic potion, they read it and think I'm indebted to them. However, I'm never in debt to any man. Some read it to look good to their fellow man (Matthew 23:26). They have their reward (Matthew 6:2).

You see, son, I search the hearts (Jeremiah 17:10). I know why people do what they do. I don't need anyone to tell me what is in man (John 2:25). You would be surprised to know how many people read My Word only because of peer *pressure* or because they think others expect it of them.

Still others read it only hoping to find errors or contradictions so they can justify not submitting to its authority. Quite a few read it to see which Scriptures they can wrest (II Peter 3:16) to fit their own wild doctrines or wicked life styles. I wrote it so that some passages appear to contradict at first glance, so those who hate Me will be caught in their own net (Psalm 35:8).

KH: Have I ever read Your Word for any of those reasons, Lord?

GOD: Nearly all of them at one time or another, son.

KH: Why should I read it, Lord?

GOD: My Word provides more things than you realize. It washes like water (Ephesians 5:26-27) and quenches the thirst (John 4:14) in those who hunger and thirst after righteousness (Matthew 5:6). My Word brings life (Proverbs 3:2) and light (Psalm 119:130). It is milk (I Peter 2:2), bread (Matthew 4:4), and meat (Hebrews 5:12-14). It is a light to your path (Psalm 119:105) and a search light for your heart (Psalm 139:23). It is your armor against the devil (Ephesians 6:11,17). It keeps you from sin (Psalm 119:11). It brings healing (Matthew 8:16). It makes you bear fruit (Matthew 13:20-23). It helps you learn of me (Matthew 11:29) to prepare you to live in my palace forever (Revelation 21:1).

KH: Do I ever read it for those reasons, Lord?

GOD: Sometimes, son, but not often enough. I've given you a lot. You have a sharp mind, good health, a loving family, a relatively free country, and lots of people who love and pray for you. You need to study to show yourself approved to Me (II Timothy 2:15). I've given you much and I will require much of you (Luke 12:48).

KH: I know, Lord. That verse scares me.

GOD: It should, son, it should. I love you. Get back to reading. I've got your back.

GOLIATH OF GATH - ONLY THE STRONGEST SURVIVE?
September 4th 2007

KH: Excuse me Mr. Goliath of Gath (GG), I couldn't help but hear you yelling and swearing (I Samuel 17:8). What seems to be the problem here?

Goliath of Gath (GG): I can't understand these stupid Jews. They think their God is the only one there is. They think He's all powerful. What a joke!

KH: Why would you say that?

GG: Their God told them—so they say—to conquer the land of Caanan—four-hundred years ago! They claim their God promised to drive out the people who lived there (Joshua 1). My people had been living there for centuries. It's our land!

KH: They did conquer the land, didn't they?

GG: Only part of it. Their God couldn't make them conquer my city of Gath (Joshua 11:22). That was over three-hundred years ago and they still can't beat us! If God told them to do it, why didn't they finish the job?

KH: Good question.

GG: I'll tell you why. Their God is weak. That's why. Why, just a few dozen years ago this puny nation of Israel didn't even have a king. They said this "God" was their king and He lived in a box they called the "ark." My father was in the battle when Israel tried to fight us (I Samuel 4:1-2). He said it was not even a fight. We beat them bad! Dad said they killed 4,000 men in just one day (I Samuel 4:2). Then, the "military leaders" of this weak little country sent men to get their God in a box to bring Him to help them win the battle (I Samuel 4:3-5). What a joke! We beat then again and took their box away from them. Ha! So much for their silly God in a box.

KH: Did your father's people keep the box?

GG: For awhile, yes, but bad things started happening in the city of Ashdod, so they brought it to my city of Gath (I Samuel 5:8).

KH: And what happened in your city?

GG: We had an outbreak of hemroids (I Samuel 5:9) so we sent the ark to another city (I Samuel 5:10). After seven months (I Samuel 6:1) our Philistine rulers sent the box back to Israel (I Samuel 6:12).

KH: Did the hemroids go away?

GG: Yes they did. So we decided there was some poison in the box. There was never any proof that God had anything to do with it. My father was a giant like me (Numbers 13:33; Deuteronomy 3:11; Joshua 12:4). He taught me to be a fighter. We know that might makes right. There is no one God to tell us right from wrong. The strongest decide right and wrong.

KH: So why are you out here yelling and swearing today.

GG: I'm cursing the stupid God of these cowardly Jews to show them the truth about their God in a box. He's nothing. If He even exists, He has no power like mine. Look at me. I'm nearly ten-feet tall!

I've got four brothers (II Samuel 21:16-22) who are as big as me. We are the dream team. We will take on anyone including that puny God of the Jews.

I've been coming out here for forty days now, yelling and cursing at these Jews and their God in a box. I told them to send me a man to fight with me, but they are all too scared (I Samuel 17:16). I challenge them every morning and evening, but there are none brave enough to fight me. They talk about how they trust their God, but they are all liars. I trust my great strength not some imaginary God in a box. They talk big, but never really put their faith into action.

KH: How long are you going to do this?

GG: I don't know. I made my challenge about thirty minutes ago and they all ran away (I Samuel 17:24) just like they always do. I'll wait a few more minutes just to rub their noses in it. I really enjoy making fun of their God and demonstrating that He doesn't exist.

KH: What are you trying to accomplish?

GG: I want to get them to give up their stupid religion and see reality. Only the strongest survive. They need to quit wasting time talking to their

God and start working out and enjoying life. They claim their God gave them some rules to live by. There are no rules from God. I break all ten of their silly rules all the time and nothing ever happens to me.

KH: Are any of your children planning on becoming University Professors to continue the tradition of mocking God and teaching others to ignore His rules?

GG: What?

KH: Never mind. I just thought I might have met some of them. Hey, Mr. Goliath, I think I see someone coming from the camp of Israel. You have a challenger.

GG: It's about time! It only took them forty days.

KH: What are the rules for the fight?

GG: No rules. Just one on one.

KH: Then why do you have two (I Samuel 17:41)?

GG: See, there you go, too. Rules are man made and mean nothing to me. Say, you're not a Jewish spy are you?

KH: No, sir. I'm Norwegian.

GG: Nor what?

KH: Never mind. It looks like your challenger is kind of small and unarmed.

GG: It's just a little boy with a rag on a string and a rock! I'll teach those Jews to mock me by sending this dog! I'll kill him and feed his body to the birds (I Samuel 17:44)! We'll see how puny their God really is.

KH: You might want to listen carefully to that boy. He may have a totally new thought to put into your head (I Samuel 17:49). I'll get out of the way now. Tell God I said "hi" when you see Him in a few minutes.

GG: Huh?

CHIEF PRIEST - LAZARUS' RESURRECTION
September 6th 2007
(based on John 12:10-11)

KH: Excuse me, Mr. Chief Priest. You sure seem angry. What is going on here?

Chief Priest (CP): We are having a meeting to discuss how to best kill Lazarus.

KH: There are plenty of ways to kill people, but I'm curious why he needs to be killed. What did he do?

CP: He won't keep his mouth shut about how Jesus raised him from the dead.

KH: It would be natural to want to tell the story about that if it's true. Was he really dead?

CP: Oh, yes, for four days! We confirmed that part of the story with many people.

KH: How can you expect a man to keep quiet about that? Wouldn't you tell people if it happened to you?

CP: I'm sure I would want to, but I would keep quiet for the greater good.

KH: What is "the greater good" you are talking about?

CP: Our plush jobs as priests! If we lose our jobs, we lose our income, retirement, insurance, security, and eventually our homes and families.

KH: I don't understand how this all ties together. What does Lazarus have to do with that?

CP: It's really simple. We get our money when people come to the temple and tithe or give offerings (Numbers 18). The more people that come, the bigger the offering.

KH: That makes sense.

CP: For several years now, attendance has been going down at the temple because more and more people are following Jesus instead. That affects our paycheck.

KH: I see.

CP: Jesus raised Lazarus from the dead and he is getting even more people converted to follow Jesus. That's why we must kill him and then kill Jesus, too.

KH: So this is all about money (I Timothy 6:10)?

CP: Mostly, but also our position, power, and ego. Plus we have a good working relationship with the Romans. We fear that this resurrection story might upset them as well.

KH: Have you considered listening to Jesus or Lazarus and getting converted yourself? After all, being raised from the dead is a big deal and shows that Jesus is not just a man, doesn't it? What if Jesus is the Messiah?

CP: We would never do that! What would we do for a living? Do you expect us to actually get a real job and work? No way! Truth means nothing compared to our paycheck and security. That's why we are having this secret meeting. We must kill Lazarus to shut him up. We need to make it look like an accident.

KH: Do you guys also have secret signs, hand-shakes, oaths, and postures?

CP: Yes, how did you know?

KH: Just a guess. Some things never change.

CP: I've got to get back to the meeting. It's better to sacrifice a few innocents to save the nation (John 11:50). We will call our plan "The Patriot Act."

BIDKAR - WICKED QUEEN JEZEBEL
September 9th 2007
(based on 2 Kings 9:25-35)

KH: Excuse me, Mr. Bidkar, you look puzzled. What seems to be bothering you?

Bidkar: My boss, Jehu, gave me a job to do. I'm supposed to bury wicked Queen Jezebel. She was thrown out of that window right above us and the horses trampled her right here about an hour ago before supper (II Kings 9:30-33).

KH: So where is she now?

Bidkar: That's what has me puzzled. All I found was her skull, her feet and the palms of her hands.

KH: That is real strange! What happened to the rest of her?

Bidkar: It looks like the dogs ate her (I Kings 21:23; II Kings 9:36).

KH: Why didn't they eat those parts?

Bidkar: That's the mystery! The more I think about it though, the more it makes sense.

KH: Tell me about your theory so far.

Bidkar: Her head was so full of wicked thoughts that even the dogs wouldn't touch it. Her feet went to wicked places and her hands caused suffering to innocent people (I Kings 18-19; 21). Dogs will eat about anything, but she was too much even for dogs!

KH: Wow! She must have been bad!

Bidkar: Oh, yeah! At least it will be a tiny grave to dig!

APOSTLE PAUL ON PRISON ENCOURAGEMENT AND DISCOURAGEMENT
September 13th 2007
(based on Acts 28:30)

KH: Hey, Paul! How are you doing?

Apostle Paul: Very well, except I'm in prison–sort of. I have lots of freedoms here in Rome. This beats all the other jails and prisons I've been in. I'm allowed to have lots of visitors (Acts 28:30) and I get to preach the kingdom of God with no restrictions (Acts 28:31). I even have my own house.

KH: What do you do in your free time?

Paul: I have lots of good books to read as well as searching the law, the prophets, and the Psalms. I write letters to churches that I helped to start. I also write to young preachers to encourage them and instruct them in the faith. I keep really busy! I've been waiting for months now to have Caesar hear my appeal. The legal system is so slow!

KH: I know exactly what you mean. Some things never change! How does your case look?

Paul: This shouldn't even be a case! I broke no laws (Acts 23:9, 29; 25:8, 10, 25; 26:31; 28:18) but there is a lot of politics involved in my case. Being innocent doesn't always mean a lot when Caesar gets you.

KH: I understand that one as well. How did you end up in prison?

Paul: It's a long story. I've been traveling and preaching in different cities for years about Jesus Christ. When I went to Jerusalem to witness to the Jews, the religious leaders didn't like what I was preaching, so they filed a lot of false charges against me (Acts 22:22; 23:6-10, 29; 24:5-9; 25:7).

The governor knew I was innocent but wanted to show favor to the Jews (Acts 24:22-27) so he left me in prison for two years (v. 27)! Do you realize how long two years is?

KH: Ah....yes, I do.

Paul: Jesus said the lawyers were under a curse because they bind heavy burdens on men, but won't touch them themselves (Luke 11:46). Prison is a heavy burden for everyone. After two years, I went back to court (Acts 25).

I could see I was getting nowhere in this court, so I appealed to Caesar (Acts 25:11). After a real wild boat ride in a storm all over the Mediterranean Sea, we wrecked on the island of Melita where we spent the winter (Acts 28:1-11). I then came to Rome a few months ago, and here I sit.

Why On Earth Did God Let This Happen... For Heaven's Sake?

KH: Do you ever get discouraged?

Paul: Oh, yes. Being locked up away from your family would discourage anyone, but God has been good to me. I've seen souls saved everywhere that I've been, but I really miss the freedom to travel and preach. Plus, I miss my family.

KH: I know just what you mean. Say, why did God allow this to happen to you?

Paul: I really wrestle with that question a lot! God hasn't told me directly, but there are several possible reasons I've thought of. It may be that I brought this on myself by not listening to the warning of the Holy Spirit. Many people who love me told me not to go to Jerusalem (Acts 20:16, 22; 21:4, 11). My heart was right. I wanted to win my fellow Jews to Christ (Romans 10:1), but God had called me to win the Gentiles (Acts 13:46; 15:7; 18:6; 22:21). Some have argued that it was a mistake for me to go to Jerusalem.

Either way, it was the Jews that sinned—not me. The question is not whether I sinned and deserve prison—but was I wise? Plus, it's too late. I'm here. Even if I was wrong, God can use it and fix it.

KH: I understand. What other reasons have you thought of?

Paul: Well, this may all be part of God's perfect plan for my life. He may want to use this to spread the Gospel even faster.

KH: How is that possible?

Paul: I was traveling and preaching a lot, but I could only be in one place at a time. Because of my being in prison, many of the brethren are now more bold and motivated to preach the gospel (Philippians 1:12-14).

Now instead of one Paul, there are hundreds of mini-Pauls out preaching. The result is more souls for the kingdom. Also, I will get to witness to Caesar and others that I probably would never have met otherwise. This all may be God's perfect will.

Another good thing that has happened is that I now have time to write letters to encourage and instruct the believers in churches all over. My letters can be copied and sent everywhere. I really think and hope and pray that they will be a blessing.

KH: So do I, Paul. So do I. What helps you most when you get discouraged?

Paul: Discouragement comes quickly and easily to anyone locked up. One day you feel up and the next, you feel down.

KH: I know. It's like a roller coaster.

Paul: A what??

KH: Never mind. I know what you mean.

Paul: Someone who has never been locked up away from their family could not possibly understand how important letters, visits, and prayers are. I see now why Jesus said to visit those in prison (Matthew 25:36) and why God's perfect law (Psalm 19:7) never called for prison as a form of punishment.

I read the Scriptures a lot. The Psalms especially bless me now. The letters I get from those who have been converted or blessed by my ministry over the years are also a great help (Proverbs 25:25). They remind me that my life was not spent on vain things and that my work is still going on for the Lord in many people's lives. I get great joy knowing that my children walk in the truth (II Corinthians 2:3; 7:13; Philippians 2:2, 17; 4:1; I Thessalonians 2:19-20).

KH: Can you imagine being locked up for a life of crime and having no memories of serving God to fall back on?

Paul: That would make it so much harder! I'm in prisons often with men like that. They are so excited to know God loves them anyway, and that it is never too late to start serving God. I guess the letters from those I've helped are one of the best sources of encouragement.

KH: I agree. Many have written to me and God uses it to really bless me and encourage me to keep going. I also read and pray a lot.

Paul: Now please don't laugh at me, Kent, but another source of help for me is reading my own letters that I have written to churches. It is almost as if God was speaking through me as I wrote (II Peter 1:21). I often go back and read my own letters and wonder, "Where did that come from?" My travel schedule was pretty hectic and having time to write blesses me, even if it blesses no one else.

KH: I think more people will be blessed than you can ever imagine, Paul!

Paul: Do you really think so?

KH: I know God will use your letters to reach more people than you could ever dream about reaching while you were out preaching.

Paul: Good! That's all I want to do with my life—win souls, teach the truths of God's Word, and encourage others to do the same.

KH: Me, too, Paul. Me, too.

Paul: I often get letters from people saying they or their church are praying for me. These letters bless me beyond words. I've seen what prayer can do! The praying church got Peter out of prison (Acts 5:18-20; 12:5)!

KH: I know. It's "not by might, nor by power, but by my spirit, saith the Lord..." (Zechariah 4:6). God will grant the prayer of a righteous man (James 5:16). I just got a letter tonight from a woman in prison who is praying for me. She said she loved watching my videos that she saw in her prison. She said, "if I had to do ninety months in prison just to be exposed to those wonderful videos...well, it's all been worth it." Thanks be to God!

Paul: I'm glad she's excited, Kent, but what's a video??

KH: Ah...never mind. I'll explain that when we get to Heaven. What other good has come from this?

Paul: Well, Timothy, my son in the faith, has had to grow up quickly. He has always loved and served God, but now he carries the entire load of my ministry. It has been hard, but he has done a great job of rising to the challenge. I'm real proud of him!

KH: I understand perfectly. The same is happening to me. God always thinks ahead and provides. Say, does it bother you that the war for souls is going on out there and you can't be out preaching like you were?

Paul: Yes and no. I'm a soldier in God's army. Winning the world for Christ is God's problem. I'm willing to go or to stay. If He needs me, He knows where I am. Jesus said, "For God so loved the world..." I don't have to love the whole world. I love God, so I deliver the message for Him. Jonah hated the people God sent him to witness to.

Apparently, God wants me to wait (Psalm 27:14; 37:7). Waiting is a very high form of worship. It shows our respect for His will and timing. He is a great King.

KH: Wow! Waiting is worship! That's a comforting thought! Thanks, I needed that.

Paul: You are welcome, Kent. For years, as I traveled, it was give, give, give of myself. Now, God is recharging me while I wait on Him.

KH: What causes you the most grief in prison, Paul?

Paul: Several things cause grief. I miss my family. It also hurts that some speak of me as an evildoer (I Peter 2:12; 3:16; 4:15). Most people, though, know how evil the Roman government is and don't believe all that is said about me. It also hurts when some believers forsake me or harm me (II Timothy 4:10, 14-16). The biggest burden is the Bildad reaction that I still get from many.

KH: What do you mean?

Paul: Remember when Jesus was asked who sinned to cause the man to be born blind (John 9:1-5)?

Well, Bildad was one of those who could not understand that the evil Job endured was not caused by Job's sin (Job 8, 18, 25). God had said three times that Job was perfect and upright (Job 1:1, 8; 2:3), but Bildad couldn't or wouldn't understand that. I guess Bildad has lots of followers alive today because they write all sorts of evil reports about me either strongly hinting or stating outright that my being in prison is proof of sin on my part. They say things like, "If you would only admit your guilt and repent, God would release you from prison."

I've examined my heart a thousand times, Kent. I may not have been wise in going to Jerusalem, but I didn't sin against God, the Jews, or Rome. I wish people would drop their little comments about it. That grieves me the most (I Peter 3:13-17). Does that make sense?

KH: Oh, Yes! I completely understand. Have any churches stopped supporting you?

Paul: Yes, some have (Philippians 4:15). That hurts too, but that is God's problem. If the case against me gets dropped or reversed and the churches won't have me back to preach, I'll just go start new ones or go where they will listen. I serve God—not men.

KH: If you win your case, are you going to sue the Jews for false arrest and the Romans for false imprisonment? They stole years of your life.

Paul: Did Job sue the Sabeans for stealing his stuff (Job 1:14-15)?

KH: Not that is recorded in Scripture.

Paul: God supplied twice as much as they stole. God can supply lots better than an earthly court (Job 42:12). No, suing would be even more of a waste of time. Maybe God sent me here to witness to someone. Maybe He sent me here to prepare the way for future persecution of His church. Jesus said we would have tribulation (John 16:33). We need to prepare for it.

KH: What should I do now while I'm in prison?

Paul: Same as I'm doing. Read, pray, witness to any who will listen and write letters.

KH: That sounds like a great plan. Thanks, Paul.

Paul: You're welcome, Kent. I'll see you in Heaven.

KH: I'll be there.

FORGIVENESS
September 20th 2007
(based on Acts 28:30)

GOD: Hey, Kent, I need you to go walk around the track a few times, now!

KH: Sure, Lord. Is there someone you want me to witness to?

GOD: You will see some people you know who are walking as well. Just walk with all of them and listen to what they are saying. I'll explain later.

Inmate #1 (IM 1): Hey Kent, did you hear about that US Attorney getting arrested last Sunday?

KH: No, what happened?

IM 1: It's all over the news. He was going to Michigan to have sex with a five-year-old! An agent posed as a mother offering her daughter and caught him.

IM 2: Did you also hear he tried to commit suicide in jail?

IM 3: He won't need to kill himself. The other inmates will take care of that! Child molesters have a short life expectancy in prison!

IM 2: He's safe for now. He's in the suicide-watch cell.

IM 3: Now the guards will get him! He's done for!

IM 1: I hope they give him the death penalty!

IM 3: I hope they arrest all the US Attorneys! Those guys lied to put me in here.

IM 2: Yeah, me too! They call it the "Justice Department." What a joke! They don't want justice; they want convictions to advance their careers.

IM 1: Those people will make up stuff, lie, or even plant evidence to convict you. I hope they all have to come here to see what they really do to families.

IM 3: Yeah, I was arrested on those !%*#! conspiracy laws. A "friend" of mine said I had sold him drugs. He lied but it got him off the hook. He didn't have to spend one day in prison! My lawyer said I should make a plea agreement. I said, "Why? The charges are bogus. He's lying. I want a trial!" The lawyer said the US Attorney was offering me thirty-six months and if I lost at trial I would get ten years! I never sold him drugs but when they told me there was a 96% chance I would lose, I agreed to the plea. Then, the judge gave me eighty-four months! I asked my lawyer what happened to the plea agreement for thirty-six months. He said they don't have to go by that! All those attorneys and judges need to spend time in here to see what it's like. I hate them!

IM 2: Yeah, they give out time like water. They must get bonuses based on how much time they give out! It's all about the money. What do you think, Kent?

KH: Well—the love of money is the root of all evil (1 Tim. 6:10) and prisons are evil. God never authorized this type of punishment. The guy needs punishment or even execution, all right, if the alleged charges are true, but not this—especially not the suicide-watch cell! I spent eight days in there in Marianna, Florida when they were moving me up here. It was the only open bed they had, or so they said. There was a concrete slab in the middle of a tiny room to sleep on. All around the slab were steel rings to chain people down. I wasn't chained, but I'm sure he is right now. It would be awful! I'll bet he's thinking of all the people he sent to prison over the years. Now he knows what prison is really like.

IM 1: Yea, it's a lot different on the inside! Jesus didn't have one good thing to say about lawyers (Luke 11:46). They love dishing out the time. Let's see how the US Attorney likes it (Galatians 6:7; Judges 1:6-7)!

GOD: OK, Kent, that's all for now. Go back to practicing the piano.

September 22 – 4:20 A.M.

KH: Lord, I can't stop thinking about that attorney chained to that bed. Please talk to him, Lord. Calm him and comfort him. Use this experience to win him to Yourself. Be with him, Lord.

GOD: Do you want me to forgive him, son?

KH: Lord, that's a tough one! You've forgiven me of an awful lot. I guess I must say yes, Lord. Please forgive him and help him come to You. Also, please bless his family. This is going to be a terrible time for his wife, his children, and his parents. I probably wouldn't have felt this way just six months ago. I was still angry at what those guys did to me and to my family. Yes, Lord, please forgive him. I don't think the system will forgive him, Lord, but I would ask You to forgive him. I also ask you to be real close to him now. I spent a lot of time kneeling by that slab feeling those iron rings and praying for Christians all over the world that are suffering right now. My mind can't handle the thought of all the pain and suffering people have gone through over the years. Please come back, Lord, and set up Your kingdom! We have pretty much ruined this world.

GOD: I will, son, when it is time.

KH: Lord, did you have me dream about that man and wake me up to see if I've changed my attitude, and become more forgiving? Was this a test?

GOD: Yes, son, I try the heart (Psalm 11:4; 26:2; 139:23; Jeremiah 9:7; 17:10).

KH: Did I pass the test, Lord? I do feel like You have changed me. I know I fail a lot of the tests You give me. Did I finally pass one?

GOD: Go back to sleep, son. You are growing but you have a long way to go.

KH: I know, Lord. I see it more and more. I love you, Lord! Goodnight.

8:20 A.M.

KH: Hey, David, did you hear about that Federal Prosecutor that was arrested for going to have sex with a five-year-old?

David: I heard about it. Why?

KH: Who was he? Do you know his name?

Michael: Sure. Here is a newspaper article about him.

KH: Wow! He is from Gulf Breeze. John David Roy Atchison.

GOD: Son, check your court records.

KH: OK, Lord. Lord, he is listed as somehow being involved in my case! He was on the team that did all this damage to me, my family, and my ministry.

GOD: Yes, son, he was. Do you still want to pray the same prayer you prayed four hours ago?

KH: Well....yes, Lord, I do. Please forgive him and save him through this experience. He will get plenty of punishment for his sin down here. He doesn't need to go to hell forever. No one should go there.

GOD: I'm not willing that any should perish, son (II Peter 3:9).

KH: I'm so glad, Lord! I deserve your judgment.

GOD: No, son, all I see when I look at you is the righteousness of Christ. Your sins are gone forever.

KH: I'm so glad, Father! You amaze me sometimes!

GOD: Sometimes?

KH: Well...I don't think about you all the time. I'll work on that.

GOD: People react many ways when they encounter someone doing evil like Attorney Atchison. Since your mind, Kent, works best with lists....

1. *They take vengeance themselves (the worst).*
2. *They get others like governments to take the revenge for them (a little better).*
3. *They pray for me to judge the evil doer (better yet).*
4. *They pray that the evil person will reap what they sow (Galatians 6:7).*
5. *They forgive them but hope they get some natural punishment.*

6. *They ask me to forgive them this time only.*
7. *They really ask me to forgive them and bless them. You were a #3 a while ago, son. This time you were a #7. That's better.*

KH: Thanks, Lord. Does this list go higher?
GOD: Oh, yes, son.

1. *They die in their place so they can be forgiven.*
2. *They send their son to die in their place so that they can be forgiven.*
3. *They forgive and forget all their sins. They justify and sanctify them, invite them to move in with them to live forever, and give them joy for all eternity. Make them your bride and marry them (Revelation 21:2, 9).*

KH: Wow! Lord, Wow! Thanks! That's what You've done!

GOD: I'll watch over Atchison, son. Thanks for praying for him. Now, you're in a building with several hundred lost men, aren't you?

KH: Yes, Lord, I sure am.

GOD: Many are vulgar, wicked, and godless. I am not in their thoughts (Psalm 10:4). Their constant profanity bothers you, doesn't it, son?

KH: Yes, Lord, it does.

GOD: Do you want me to judge them or forgive them?

KH: I understand, Lord. They can only be forgiven through the blood of Christ. I had better go tell them about it, hadn't I?

GOD: Yes, son. It will be a fearful thing if they face me with their sin (Hebrews 10:31). Thank you, son, for not rejoicing over this man's fall (Proverbs 24:17). Help your fellow Christians learn this also.

KH: OK, Lord, I'll try. I love you, Lord.

GOD: I love you too, son. Get to work. I've got your back.

HUR - FANAFI (FIND A NEED AND FILL IT)
September 20th 2007
(based on Exodus 17:8-13)

KH: Excuse me, Mr. Hur, what is going on here?

Hur: I'm holding up Moses' arm. His brother Aaron is holding the other one.

KH: Hi, Aaron.

Aaron: Hi, Kent. I'd shake your hand, but I can't let go right now.

KH: I understand. So, Mr. Hur, can you explain why you are holding up his arm?

Hur: Well, God led us out of Egypt about two months ago. It was so incredible! No one would have ever dreamed that the most powerful nation on earth would ever let its captives go, but God did it! We crossed the Gulf of Aqaba and have been following the Lord in this wilderness of Arabia for several weeks (Exodus 16:1; Galatians 4:25). We came here to Rephidim (Exodus 17:1) but had no water; so the people complained like they always do, and God worked a great miracle to provide it.

KH: How did God get enough water out here in the desert for all of you? There sure are a lot of people.

Hur: We haven't counted, but our guess is that there are about two million people plus lots of animals. It takes a lot of water to satisfy this crowd!

KH: I'll say! So how did God do it?

Hur: I doubt you would believe me if I told you.

KH: Try me. I might.

Hur: Well, do you see this rod Moses is holding up?

KH: Yes, it looks like a regular walking stick.

Hur: God told Moses to hit that big rock over on that hill to your right. When Moses hit it with this rod, the rock split in two—and water came gushing out in a river (Exodus 17:5-6).

KH: I see the river now. I see the split in the rock, too. Wow! That rock is huge!

Hur: That just happened a few days ago. Water in the desert is worth more than gold; so the children of Amalek attacked us yesterday to get the water for themselves (Exodus 17:8).

KH: That makes sense. When God blesses you, there are always those who want to steal your blessing rather than get their own. Some things never change.

Hur: Anyway, Moses told Joshua to choose men to go fight with Amalek (Exodus 17:9) while the three of us came up here on the hill to watch and direct the battle. As long as Moses holds up this rod, the children of Israel win (Exodus 17:11). He did really well holding it up by himself for quite a while, but he's only human, you know. Eventually, anyone's arms would get tired (Exodus 17:12).

KH: That's for sure. The anaerobic respiration of glycogen and blood glucose produces a lactic acid buildup in the deltoid, triceps, and flexors that eventually crosses the lactate threshold causing muscle fatigue and inevitable failure at some point. It happens to everyone.

Hur: What???

KH: Ah...his arms got tired.

Hur: Right...I think! Anyway, Aaron and I could see right away that he needed help; so we moved this big rock over here for him to sit on and each of us started holding up an arm. We've been doing this nearly all day (Exodus 17:12).

KH: Did God tell you to help him?

Hur: God doesn't need to tell us every little detail in life. Some things are just obvious. If a man of God is tired, discouraged, or needs help, you just do it, that's all.

KH: Boy! I wish everyone felt that way. How's the battle going?

Hur: You can see for yourself. We are beating them really badly! It looks like it's almost over now. I came up here with Moses just to be near him and to help him any way that I could. I didn't do much and I sure don't understand it all, but holding up his arms seems to have been important to God.

KH: It is, Hur. It is. Just the sight of Moses holding up that rod inspires the people down there. The rod must remind them of God providing a way across the sea (Exodus 14:16) and providing water from the rock (Exodus 17:5).

Hur: That's the same rod that turned to a snake (Exodus 4:2-4) and did other signs and wonders of God (Exodus 4:17; 7:9, 20; 8:5,16; 9:22; 10:13).

KH: It's amazing that God can use a simple stick to deliver His people and provide water from a rock in a desert!

Hur: All He needs are servants willing to use whatever they have in their hands already. Lots of people think they can't serve God until they get something other than what they already have.

KH: That stick doesn't look heavy enough to require three men to hold it up.

Hur: Oh, it's not heavy, but even little things will wear you out after a while.

KH: That's so true! Most people don't understand that simple truth.

Hur: I knew months ago that God had called Moses to deliver us out of Egypt. I told God right then that I'd be willing to help His leader any way that I could. God impressed on me to just stay near Moses and be alert for any little thing I could do to help.

> *"Here Moses, take a drink of water."*

Moses: Thanks, Hur. How did you know I was thirsty before I even asked?

Hur: I try to watch your face and focus on your needs. I know you are not perfect, Moses, but you are God's man called for this job; and I'm here to help.

Moses: Thanks, Hur. God will bless you.

KH: God needs more people with your servant's heart, Hur. Most people want the glamorous jobs, not the "little" jobs that bring no glory to themselves personally.

Hur: FANAFI! That's my motto.

KH: What's FANAFI?

Hur: Find A Need And Fill It.

KH: You will always have a job with that motto!

Hur: I know. The world is full of needs for God's kingdom. I don't understand how anyone can be bored in this life.

KH: Me either! Are you passing this motto on to your children?

Hur: I'm trying. My grandson, Bezaleel, seems not only to want to help the Lord's cause, but he is also very talented. I hope God will use him someday.

KH: Oh, He will, Hur. He will (Exodus 31:2-5; 35:30-36:7)! Everyone should learn all they can in a variety of subjects so they can be used of God anywhere He may send them.

Hur: Hey, Kent, would you mind holding this arm while I get supper ready.

KH: I'd be honored, Hur, more than you can imagine.

DISCOURAGEMENT - SATAN'S FAVORITE TOOL!
September 27th 2007
(based on Acts 28:30)

GOD: Good morning, son!

KH: Good morning, Lord. What time is it?

GOD: Time means nothing to me, son. I'm eternal (1 Timothy 1:17). To you, it's 4:00 a.m.

KH: Lord—why can't You wait until 6:30 or 7:00 to wake me up?

GOD: I could, son, but you tend to get busy with other things and don't really focus on Me. I want your undivided attention.

KH: Well—you've got it, Lord—what there is of it anyway. What would You like me to do?

GOD: You've been through the valley of discouragement for several weeks now, son. I sent you there to teach you some things.

KH: I'm ready to learn, Lord, especially if it means I can get out of here and go home.

GOD: Do you think any of the other 530 men in here with you ever get discouraged?

KH: Oh, yes, Lord! Some are in that valley all the time, some part of the time, and probably everyone goes to that valley once in a while.

GOD: It is time for you to try the "all-call" feature of knee-mail.

KH: The what?

GOD: ALL CALL. Knee-mail reaches everyone, everywhere at any time, does it not?

KH: Yes, Lord. I have loved using it!

GOD: Have any people in the Bible ever faced prison or discouragement?

KH: Oh, yes, Lord, nearly all of them.

GOD: Did they overcome it?

KH: Most of them, Lord. I don't know about Jonah.

GOD: He was a tough case. Send an "ALL CALL" to find out different ways they overcame discouragement (I Corinthians 10:11). I think you will find the answer right in my Word.

KH: OK, Lord—ALL CALL—Can anyone give me advice on how to overcome discouragement, especially when being confined against your will?

Noah: I'll be glad to help, Kent. I was one of the first. I was confined in a very wicked world. Nobody wanted to serve God in my day! It was very discouraging to try to serve God when I was surrounded every day by cursing, violence, and immorality (Genesis 6:5).

KH: That sounds just like today (II Peter 3:3)! So what helped you overcome discouragement, Noah?

Noah: Three things. First—preparation. I knew a flood was coming so I spent a lot of time building the ark. Ever since Adam, work has been great therapy (Genesis 3:17). The work of building the ark with my family was also a wonderful bonding time. I recommend a family project. Even those locked away from family can still do this.

KH: Yes, that's true. I send my grandkids stories I write and stamps for their stamp collection.

Noah: What's a stamp?

KH: Uhhh, never mind. Let's just say that even prisoners can still work on projects with their families. You said there were three things, what else?

Noah: Yes, second is preaching. Telling others about the Lord, even if they aren't listening, is good to help overcome discouragement. God is not willing that any should perish (II Peter 3:9) and I get real satisfaction knowing that God is pleased with my work even if no one gets saved. I want to hear Him say "Well done" (Matthew 25:21).

The third thing is prayer. I spend time in prayer. When I look at the wicked world around me, I get discouraged (Matthew 14:30); but when I stay focused on God, I get uplifted. It really helps.

KH: Thanks, Noah. That's great advice!

Job: Hey, Kent, I'll go next. I had a serious case of discouragement. I even wished I would die (Job 3)! Everything went wrong for me. I went totally broke in one day. All ten of my children died and even my wife turned against me—all in just a few days. My friends only made it worse with their false accusations.

KH: So what helped you?

Job: Well, three things. I knew I had brought the sacrifice God required for my sin so I consistently maintained my integrity (Job 2:3; 27:5) in spite of the speeches I was hearing. I also trusted God to do right. I knew He was testing me and I would come forth as gold (Job 23:10). So, my advice is the following:

1. *Don't listen to critics.*
2. *Maintain your integrity*
3. *Keep trusting God.*

KH: Thanks, Job, that's very helpful.

Abram: Hey, Kent, let me pop in here with my two shekels worth. I've got some great advice on what NOT to do to overcome discouragement. God promised my wife and me a son (Gen 15:5-6) but I got discouraged with the long wait for God to fulfill the promise so I found another woman. I thought a younger woman would help me overcome my discouragement (Genesis 16:16).

KH: Did it help?

Abram: No! It was a big, big, big mistake! Now I have lots of friction in what used to be a happy family (Genesis 17, 21). My wife hates the new woman and her son (Genesis 21:10). I have a feeling this mistake is going to cost me for the rest of my life.

KH: Cost you? Your mistake is costing me $3.00 a gallon for gas!

Abram: What's a dollar, and what is gas?

KH: That's a lo-o-o-o-ng story. Let's just say that your mistake will cost everyone in the world for four thousand years!

Abram: Wow! I am so sorry! Anyway, my advice on how to overcome discouragement is:

1. *Believe God*
2. *Wait on God.*
3. *Do not get involved with other women!*

KH: If the grass looks greener on the other side of the fence, the guy has a huge water bill or it is artificial turf!

Abram: It's what?

KH: Never mind. Thanks for the advice.

Lot: Hey, Kent, my uncle Abram is right. Let me add my shekel's worth. I was real disgusted with the wickedness in my city (II Peter 2:7), but I stayed in the city anyway. Big mistake! I was attracted to it because of the green grass (Genesis 13:10), and I didn't check the morals of the people where I would raise my children. Now I have lost them all. My two oldest daughters laughed at me when I tried to warn them of God's judgment and were burned up with Sodom (Genesis 19:14). In spite of God's command not to look back, my wife had to have one last look at Sodom and died (Genesis 19:26). My two youngest daughters got me drunk and are now both pregnant by me, their own father.

I knew the school in Sodom taught sex education starting in K-5 but I never dreamed how their evil influence would destroy my family (Genesis 19:30-38). When I first got discouraged with the sin, I should have left town (Proverbs 19:27).

My advice:

> 1. *Don't hang around sinners (Psalm 1:1).*
> 2. *Don't think the easy way is the best way. I chose the plain. Abram chose the mountains.*
> 3. *Choosing the hard way is sometimes the best way. Life has lots of valleys to go through but the mountaintop experience makes them worthwhile.*

KH: Thanks, that helps a "lot."

Joseph: Good advice, Lot. Sometimes you can't get away from all the sin. Kent is in prison like I was (Genesis 39:20). Here is my advice. I was pretty down when my own brothers sold me into slavery (Genesis 37:27)! Who wouldn't be? I knew God was with me and He was too good to make a mistake so I decided to work hard wherever I was and to try to do right.

Most slaves do the minimum amount of work for their master. I worked hard as if I was working for God Himself and He blessed me. My master Potiphar made me the overseer of his entire business (Genesis 39:1-6)!

I overcame discouragement with hard work. Noah told you the same thing. Get a project to do and pour yourself into it.

When my master's wife tried to seduce me and lied about me (Genesis 39:7-20), I was thrown into prison. There, I did the same thing. I worked hard and looked for ways to improve the prison. I gave them many ideas to save money and make prison life better for both prisoners and guards. Before long, I was promoted to prison manager (Genesis 39:21-14) and always maintained my innocence (Genesis 40:15).

God has blessed in ways I never dreamed (Genesis 41:37-45)! My advice: help others, work hard, trust God, and bloom where you are planted. You can't get out without favor from the king. Getting things done brings real sweetness and peace to the soul (Proverbs 13:19)!

KH: Thanks, Joseph. That's great advice!

David: Hey, Kent, I was very discouraged when the Amalekites burned my entire town, then stole all my stuff and my two wives (I Samuel 30:1-6). To make it worse, my own friends and co-workers were talking of stoning me! My world totally changed in one day!

KH: Boy do I know that feeling! What did you do?

David: The only place I found any encouragement was in the Lord (I Samuel 30:6). I had to encourage myself since no one else was doing it for me. I met with a godly brother (I Samuel 30:7) and prayed about what to do.

God told me to go after the ones who did this wrong (I Samuel 30:8). So we planned, prepared and proceeded on the offensive to take back what had been stolen.

My advice: *encourage yourself and go on the offense! I did that with a lion, a bear, and Goliath (I Samuel 17). I also sing and play music. Music is a gift from God that soothes the spirit.*

KH: It sure worked great with King Kong in that old movie!

David: A what?

KH: Never mind. I'll explain later. Thanks, David!

Elijah: Hey, Kent, let me tell you what helped me. I was a real famous prophet of the Lord. I even killed 850 false prophets (I Kings 18:19), called down fire from Heaven (I Kings 18:38), and prayed down rain to break a three-year drought! But, when wicked Queen Jezebel vowed to kill me, there are no words to describe how discouraged and scared I was! I ran for 150 miles (I Kings 19:3), sat under a juniper tree, and asked God to kill me (I Kings 19:4)! God saw my need and sent an angel to minister just what I needed.

KH: And what was that?

Elijah: Rest, refreshment, and a reminder. Even though God had used me greatly in the past, I was so discouraged! I was also exhausted after my long trip running away from Jezebel. Somehow being exhausted really enhances discouragement. I slept a long time and then woke up to find food ready to eat! Then I slept even more (I Kings 19:5-7). Sleeping and getting proper nourishment really revives your spirits! The refreshment was critical to my mental well-being as well. Good healthy food is essential.

KH: That is so true. Some people are out of shape, fill up on junk food like coke, pizza, and twinkies, and then wonder why they are depressed.

Elijah: They eat what?

KH: Never mind. Let's just say that I understand.

Elijah: Some people do not seem to realize that their spirit has to live in their body! When the body's needs are met, it revives the spirit. The angel from God knew exactly what to give me.

Did you notice how important resting is to God in the Bible? He ordered his people, the Jews, to take a Sabbath Day of rest every week (Exodus 20:8), a whole year off every seven years (Leviticus 25:4), and another year of rest every fifty years (Leviticus 25:11)! Plus, He ordered plenty of feasts and parties (Leviticus 23)! God wants us to rest and to eat. Noah's name even means rest.

KH: Wow! They had lots of time to worship God when they rested!

Elijah: I almost cry thinking about it. It was a cake on the coals of fire and a cruse of water. It was the perfect reminder of how God provided for me in the past. The cake and cruse reminded me of two great miracles God did for me. He fed me at the brook (I Kings 17:6) and at the widow woman's house (I Kings 17:12-16).

It was as if God was saying, "Hey there, my exhausted, discouraged prophet, when will you learn to trust Me?" Didn't I provide for you before? What are you worried about?"

I tell you what, Kent, that cruse by the coals of fire looked exactly like the one that never ran out of oil at the widow woman's house (1 Kings 17:16). God really worked on my heart!

I did not quite get the message, though. I was still scared, so I ran another 180 miles further south all the way to Mt. Sinai in Arabia (I Kings 19:8). That forty-day long trip made me even more discouraged! I thought I was the only one left serving God (I Kings 19:10). God was so-o-o-o good to me. He came to me again. Twice He asked me what I was doing way down there (I Kings 19:9,13). I can still hear that question from God, "What doest thou here, Elijah?"

I think there are several meanings to the question. He wasn't just asking about my location. The "here" referred to my state of mind. Why was I scared of one wicked woman? Why was I doubting His protection and provision? Why wasn't I out preaching?

There in front of that cave God gave me a new job to do for Him (I Kings 19:15). It felt great to be doing God's business again! Here is my advice to fight discouragement:

1. *Sleep plenty!*
2. *Eat healthy.*
3. *Remember how God provided in the past. I recommend a diary or journal. It really helps to go back and read it when Satan tries to get you down.*
4. *Keep visual reminders like the cruse.*
5. *Don't think you are the only one serving God or suffering persecution.*
6. *Always listen to the still, small voice of God.*
7. *Get a job to do for God.*

KH: Great advice, Elijah. That will help. It really helps me to know that you are just a regular guy with the same passions and problems that I face (James 5:17-18).

Daniel: Hey, Kent, I agree with Elijah. The healthy diet is critical! I faced a real opportunity for discouragement. I was taken captive to Babylon, where they changed my name, clothes, and customs (Daniel 1:7) and made me a eunuch. All my plans of marriage, children, and grandchildren were gone. That was discouraging!

The first thing that I did was request a diet of all vegetables and water. After only ten days, everyone could see the difference it made. I felt better and was more alert. I studied hard (Daniel 1:17) and decided the best thing I could do to serve God here, was to work hard at whatever job I was given. Here is my advice:

1. *Eat right.*
2. *Work hard.*
3. *Forget what's done and don't dwell in the past.*
4. *Learn a new language and culture.*
5. *Serve God.*

KH: Thanks, Daniel, for that great advice!

Paul: Hey, Kent, I've been beaten, imprisoned, threatened, shipwrecked, robbed, weary, in pain, cold, hungry, and naked (II Corinthians 11:23-33). I'll be glad to tell you how I keep out of the valley of discouragement.

KH: Oh, please do, Paul!

Paul: I sing and praise God even if I'm in pain or freezing (Acts 16:25). I witness to everyone I meet and I write lots of letters to teach or encourage others. Writing is great therapy and my own letters even encourage me as I reread them.

KH: I know just what you mean.

Paul: While I'm locked up (which is quite often), I try to make a few converts among the prisoners or staff and start discipling them. That causes me to forget my own problems and lifts my spirits.

I also love getting letters from people I've helped over the years. I keep the letters and read them again when Satan tries to discourage me. It reminds me that my labor has not been in vain.

KH: Thank you, Paul, your letters are still helping millions!

Andrew: Hey Kent, I'd like to add one more thing. While I was with Jesus, my fellow disciple, Thomas, was always a pessimist. He could see the worst in every situation (John 11:16; 14:5; 20:25). I knew he loved Jesus but I couldn't stand to be around his negative spirit. I found myself getting pulled down as well. I learned to avoid him as much as I could. After the resurrection when he saw the nail prints in Jesus' hands, he seemed to change (John 20:28). Now we get along fine. My advice—stay away from negative people!

KH: Thanks, Andrew.

Esther: Hey, Kent, can a woman give advice too?

KH: Sure, please do!

Esther: I was taken away from my homeland as a child. Both my parents died; so my cousin raised me. God made me beautiful so I was forced to enter a "beauty contest" and was selected to be queen. I had to marry a man who already had hundreds of wives. It was discouraging to feel that I was only wanted for my body.

God showed me that I was missing the bigger picture! God used my captivity, tragedy, and then position as queen to save millions of His people from extermination (Esther 3-10). My advice is this. Rather than be discouraged, wait and see if there is a much bigger picture for which God is using you. I stayed faithful to God and did the one thing that I could do—focus on pleasing my husband the king.

KH: During the early years of your marriage, didn't your husband lead the navy against Greece and suffer a serious defeat?

Esther: Yes, he did, but I never said one word to him about it. He got plenty of advice and criticism from others. I lived in a system with hundreds of jealous women and people trying to tell the king what to do or what he should have done. I ignored everything and focused on loving and supporting my husband. God used it for good.

KH: He always does (Romans 8:28). Thanks.

GOD: Well, son, has this helped?

KH: Yes, Lord. It has. It seems like everyone had good reasons to get discouraged if they wanted to.

GOD: Yes, son, bad things happen to good people. I allow it for their good, for My glory, and to see how they will react.

KH: How am I doing, Lord?

GOD: You are all over the charts, son! You have good moments and bad moments. Overall, you are getting better. I do not think you are ready to handle real persecution, though.

KH: I know, Lord. I am sorry. I read Fox's Book of Martyrs and stories in Voice of the Martyrs, and I feel like such a wimp as a Christian. So many believers today suffer for their faith! I'm thankful for the freedom I have and feel ashamed that I don't do more for You. I see now that this prison time is precious and should not be wasted.

GOD: Son, you will look back on this as one of the best things that ever happened to you. Esther spent a full year soaking in oils to prepare for the king's presence. You need to soak in My Word and presence, son. I am all you need. David saw the heathen prosper and saw his own problems and couldn't understand—until he went into My sanctuary (Psalm 73:17).

There are millions of My children in prison or bad situations right now around the world. I hear their cry (Exodus 2:23-24). I'm coming to fix everything (Daniel 2:44). I'm not nervous and I'm never late. Spend time with My children, son. I love it when you tell others about Me and My Word (Malachi 3:16).

KH: And I love doing it, Lord! I just want my freedom back to finish telling everyone in the world about Your creation and salvation. I didn't even get to one-fourth of the countries yet.

GOD: It will come, son; so relax. Right now we need to patch a few leaks. Do you remember the little Honda three-wheeler you had for your son, Eric?

KH: Yes, Lord, one of the tires had about a dozen plugs in it, and it still went flat every five days. I couldn't afford a new one so I kept plugging it. He loved riding it though and still has the scar on his lip to prove it.

GOD: You are like that tire, son. You go flat easily. Elijah had the same problem. You both get discouraged in My work.

KH: I know, Lord. I am sorry. At least I'm still willing and wanting to keep rolling for you, Lord, if You'll have me. Remember that You choose the weak and foolish things to do Your work so only You get the glory (I Corinthians 1:26-31).

GOD: Good answer, son! That is the spirit I want to see. I'll keep you pumped up and rolling while I work on those leaks—all at the same time.

KH: Thank you, Lord. You are great!

GOD: I am the best, son. Now, quit crying and start using that advice you just got from the "ALL CALL." Don't forget that I sent you to prison for more than just you. There are over forty lost men watching you like a hawk. It takes a while for you to prove you are genuine to them. I brought you there for them. They are coming around. George is only one. Thanks for sharing My Word with him yesterday. No one has ever shared the simple plan of salvation with him. He saw your tender heart and tears and is under deep conviction right now. Thanks for letting Me put you in prison to reach him.

KH: Lord, You know I want to go home but thanks for sending him. I loved witnessing to him. Please send more.

GOD: Oh, I will, son. I will. People in and out of the prison are watching. Rest in Me. I've got your back.

JACOB, WHY ARE YOU STILL IN EGYPT?
October 9th 2007
(based on Genesis 46:1 – 47:28)

KH: Hey, Jacob! You look relaxed. You have had a long life, haven't you?

Jacob: Oh, yes! God has been good. I'm 147 years old. My thirteen children have given me more grandkids than I can count. All my needs are met by my son Joseph. He's the Vice-Pharoah here in Egypt. I'm content and ready to die.

KH: May I ask you a few questions?

Jacob: Sure, go ahead.

KH: How did you end up in Egypt?

Jacob: I brought the family here seventeen years ago because of a great famine in the land. My son, Joseph really rescued us from starvation. There were about seventy of us in the family at that time (Genesis 46:27).

KH: How long did the famine last?

Jacob: It lasted seven years all together. We came down here in the second year. So six years after we got to Egypt, it was over.

KH: Since God promised the land of Canaan to your grandfather Abraham (Genesis 13:15), why didn't you go back when the famine was over eleven years ago? Why are you still in Egypt?

Jacob: That's a hard question to answer. I probably should have. It would not be easy to move now. There are several hundred of us. We all have nice houses, good jobs, plenty of food (Numbers 11:5), and good weather. I know God really wants us up there, but that's a long hard walk!

KH: Yes, I understand. Many people don't follow God's calling to the mission field or full-time service for Him because of the comforts of this world (Matthew 4:19; II Timothy 4:10; I John 2:15). Many are called but few obey (Matthew 22:14).

Jacob: You are making me feel kind of bad about staying here. It's not like we are doing wickedly, you know. We worship God here and give to missionaries. We still maintain our heritage. We won't let too much of Egypt rub off on us.

KH: Won't it just get harder to go back every year?

Jacob: Well...that's a good point. I don't know how to answer that one. I know I'm the spiritual leader, but there is no hurry to go back. It's comfortable here.

KH: Will God have to make it uncomfortable to get you to do His will?

Jacob: Boy! Your questions pierce my heart! I know I've always looked for ways to get things the easy way. I swapped a bowl of soup for a double portion of my father's inheritance (Genesis 25:29-34). Then I tricked my dad into giving me the blessing (Genesis 27). Years later I basically stole the flocks from my father-in-law Laban (Genesis 30:32-43).

KH: Didn't you also deceive your brother, Esau, again when he offered to lead you home, but you went another way to avoid him (Genesis 33:17)?

Jacob: Well...maybe a little bit.

KH: I noticed that you also didn't defend your only daughter when she was defiled. You let your sons do it (Genesis 34:5).

Jacob: Well...it was a lot easier just to drop the issue. I guess I do always take the easy road, don't I?

KH: It looks that way to me. Don't you think staying in Egypt eleven years after the famine is another example of this?

Jacob: I guess I never thought about it like that. After all, my needs are all being met right here.

KH: But God called your family to Canaan. I've met a lot of people who seem perfectly willing to sacrifice the future of their family as long as they get to experience pleasure and comfort. Would it bother you if you knew that your eleven years of easy life would cost thousands of your family members great pain and suffering for hundreds of years?

Jacob: Well...yes, a little bit. But not enough to get me to move.

KH: I'm sure glad that George Washington, Patrick Henry, and thousands of other patriots who founded my country didn't feel that way.

Jacob: Who are you talking about?

KH: Never mind. That's a long story. It seems to me that people who take drugs, smoke cigarettes, drink alcohol, and commit adultery think the same way you do.

Jacob: Smoke what?

KH: Never mind. Hey, Jacob, how about if I help you pack and move? Would you go then?

Jacob: Maybe later. Not now.

AZOR - LOVING EARTHLY WEALTH
October 10th 2007
(based on Matthew 19:16-26, Mark 10:17-22 and Luke 18:18-23)

KH: Excuse me, sir. This is a fine boat you have here!

Azor: Well, thank you, Kent. I like it.

KH: It looks like the biggest one on the Sea of Galilee!

Azor: It is. She cost about a thousand denarius ($80,000.00). It's the top of the line.

KH: Do you live near here?

Azor: Yes. That's my house up there on the hill.

KH: Isn't that the mansion where the governor of this region lives?

Azor: Yes. I am the governor.

KH: Wow! I've heard you have lots of money.

Azor: Oh, I've got plenty to meet my needs. I decided as a young man to work hard and earn as much money as I could. I've lived around here all my life and always wanted to build a nice house on that hill overlooking the Sea of Galilee.

KH: Didn't Jesus do a lot of His earthly ministry around here about twenty-five years ago?

Azor: Yes, He did.

KH: Did you ever get to hear Him preach?

Azor: Well...sort of...from a distance you might say. I heard some of his message as I was doing business one day. He had quite a crowd following him as usual.

I also saw him feed nearly 20,000 people one day with only five loaves and two fishes. It happened on that grassy slope over there to the right. People talked about that day for many years afterwards.

KH: Did you ever actually talk to Jesus?

Azor: Yes, one time, but only for a few minutes (Matthew 19:16-26). I was just in my thirties, but was already doing real well financially and politically.

KH: What did you talk to Jesus about?

Azor: I was rich but still felt pretty unfulfilled. I had heard a lot of real excited people talk about Jesus; so I actually ran to see Him. I asked Him what good thing I had to do to inherit eternal life.

KH: What did He tell you?

Azor: He told me to keep the commandments so I asked Him which ones. He only listed six of the ten Moses gave us in the Torah. They were the ones that deal with man's relation to his fellow man (Matthew 19:18-19). I told Him that I had kept all of those but still felt like something was missing.

That's when he told me to sell everything I had, give it to the poor, and follow Him (Mark 10:21)!

KH: So did you do it?

Azor: No way! I was rich even then. If the poor want money, they can work for it like I did. I was pretty sad. I wouldn't have minded if He had said give some money, but He wanted it all!! I couldn't believe He would even suggest such a crazy idea (Mark 10:22)! That was many years ago now. I decided that day to really climb the political ladder and make money.

I have endeavored to give much to the poor and to worthy causes. I think God will let me into Heaven.

KH: Have you thought anymore about what Jesus told you to do?

Azor: Almost every day of my life! His words still haunt me. I just can't believe that God would require anyone to sell everything he owned and give it away in order to go to Heaven!

KH: I don't think He does. Maybe He told that to you because He saw your love of money was keeping you from obeying the other four commandments.

Azor: I thought about that. That's why I give so much money away to charities. I built the synagogue at Bethsaida. From the deck around my house, I can see the grassy spot where He fed all those people. He did a lot of things around this lake. People around here still talk about Him all the time. A few of his disciples are still alive and come up here to give tours or fishing trips once in a while.

I give charity boat trips to under-privileged children and gave land for the cemetery at Capernaum. I'm very civic-minded but it never seems to satisfy the pain in my heart.

KH: Do you ever wish you would have followed Jesus that day?

Azor: Well...sometimes. I think about His words a lot. I probably should have done what he said.

KH: Are you happy?

Azor: I've had the best of everything. My children went to the best schools. I have the best clothes. I eat the finest food and live in the biggest house. I have the biggest boat on the lake and my wife shops at the elite stores, but...no—I'm not happy in life. I missed God's calling on my life twenty-five years ago.

KH: It's not too late! You can still do what Jesus said. He is gone, but His disciples are going all over starting churches and preaching. Paul is trying to raise money now for his third missionary journey to Macedonia and Achaia. You could just sell this boat and finance the entire trip yourself. Think about the rewards in Heaven!

Azor: That sounds tempting but...I'm pretty comfortable with where I am. I like my boat (Matthew 13:22; Mark 10:23; Luke 8:14; James 5:2).

KH: Have you thought about what happens to you when you die (Hebrews 9:27)?

Azor: I try not to think about that.

YOUNG FATHER - WALKING WITH GOD; FAMILY DEVOTIONS
October 14th 2007
(based on Acts 28:30)

GOD: Hey, Son! Let's go for a walk.

KH: Sure, Lord! Where to?

GOD: Just hold my hand, Son. Does it matter where we go?

KH: No, Father. I love to walk with You. Please teach me things.

GOD: I love to do just that, Son. I loved walking and talking with Adam and Eve in the garden before they sinned (Genesis 3:8). I walked among my people as they camped (Deuteronomy 23:14). I walked with Shadrach, Meshach, and Abednego in the fire (Daniel 3:25). I even walked on the water to rescue some scared children of Mine (Matthew 14:25). I love walking with My children and teaching them (Luke 24:13-32). I created you to fellowship with Me but you get distracted so easily.

KH: I'm sorry, Lord. I do love walking with You. Where are we, Lord?

GOD: Do you recognize this place, Son?

KH: It looks familiar, Lord, but it's too dark to make it out. Do I know that man walking with his children?

GOD: Just watch and listen, Son.

Young Father (YF): Hey, kids! Shine your flashlights over here! Hurry!

Four-Year-Old Son: What is it, Daddy?

YF: It's a huge moth! Look at the beautiful green wings. It's called a luna moth. It is one of the biggest moths that God made. Isn't it pretty?

Three-Year-Old Daughter: Does it bite, Daddy?

YF: No-o-o-o-o. Moths can't bite. Do you see those things on his head that look like feathers?

Four-Year-Old Son: I see them, Daddy. What are they?

YF: Those are his antennae. That is how they hear and smell!

Five-Year-Old Son: Why is he on the street, Daddy?

YF: I don't know, Son. But this is not a good place for him to sleep. A car might come by and smash him flat. You should never play in the street!

Four-Year-Old Son: Can we pick him up?

YF: Sure, Son. Go ahead. Put your hand down flat in front of him, so he can walk up on it.

Four-Year-Old Son: I'm scared he will bite me!

YF: Here, I'll pick him up to show you.

Five-Year-Old Son: You got him, Daddy! You got him!

Four-Year-Old Son: Can I hold him?

YF: Yes, sir. Hold real still so we don't scare him. Good job, Son. Isn't God smart! He made the most amazing world for us to study! I love Him so-o-o-o-o much! I want you kids to always love Him, too. Let's put him on a tree over here. OK, kids, let's go have devotions!

All Three Kids: Yea!!! Can we have raisins tonight?

Three-Year-Old Daughter: I want to ride the donkey!

Four-Year-Old Son: I want to be the robber!

Five-Year-Old Son: Can I be the one who helps the man going down to Jericho?

YF: Everybody hold hands and stay close to me in case a car comes.

KH: Lord, do they all live in that tiny house?

GOD: Yes, son. It's eight hundred square feet of love and joy. Those children love to learn about My Word and they really love to go for walks every night with their mommy and daddy. Their daddy loves teaching them things.

KH: I see that. Are they poor?

GOD: In the eyes of the world; yes, Son, but they are rich in the things that really matter.

KH: Can I talk with that young father, Lord?

GOD: Yes. Go ahead.

KH: Excuse me, young man; this is quite a little family you have here!

YF: I know! I wish I had ten. God has been so good to me! I love our nightly walks. We always stop and learn about God's amazing creation. We study bugs, birds, plants, rocks, trees, toads, and anything else that comes along.

KH: The kids seem to enjoy it.

YF: Oh, they do! I pray so hard that they will always love God and serve Him with their lives. I try to make learning about God fun. I want their relationship with God the Father to be as real as taking a walk with Dad.

KH: Do you do this every night?

YF: If possible. I want to build a love for God in their hearts.

KH: Isn't it crowded in that tiny house?

YF: Oh...cozy would be a better word. We are a really close family. God has always provided for us.

KH: Are you happy?

YF: If I were any happier, I'd burst! I love my wife. I love my teaching job. I love my kids. They are close in age which was really difficult during the diaper stage, but now with that stage over; they are easier to handle. They love me and don't have any idea how poor we are.

KH: It's pretty dark but this place looks familiar. Where are we?

YF: This is 804 Everett Street, Longview, Texas, sir.

KH: What year is it?

YF: It's 1982, sir. Are you OK?

KH: I'll be fine. I think I know you.

YF: I'm Kent Hovind, sir. I don't recall ever meeting you. Are you from around here?

KH: Oh...I used to live around here years ago, but that's a long story!

YF: I need to go in now, sir. Every night we act out Bible stories for family devotions and then ask questions to see what they have learned. If they answer the question right, they get a prize. Tonight, it's raisins. I've only got one box, but you are welcome to join us. We've had hundreds of people join us for family devotions to see how we teach our kids the Bible. It's real fun!

KH: No, not tonight. Thanks so much for asking. I need to go for a walk with my dad right now. He loves to teach me things as well. Good night, Kent. Enjoy your family. They grow up fast.

YF: Good night, sir. Enjoy your walk with your dad. Ah...sir? I didn't get your name.

KH: You wouldn't believe me if I told you, Kent. We'll meet again one day and I'll explain.

KH: God? Please hold my hand and walk with me. I don't understand why all this happened to me, Lord. Please teach me tonight.

GOD: Oh, Son, it would be My pleasure! Let's walk on a while. I've got more to teach you than you could ever imagine!

MALCHUS - BELIEF DURING PERSECUTION
October 28th 2007
(based on John 18:10 and Acts 9:1-2)

John 18:10 Then Simon Peter having a sword drew it, and smote the high priest's servant, and cut off his right ear. The servant's name was Malchus.

Acts 9:1-2 And Saul, yet breathing out threatening and slaughter against the disciples of the Lord, went unto the high priest, And desired of him letters to Damascus to the synagogues, that if he found any of this way, whether they were men or women, he might bring them bound unto Jerusalem.

(At Acts 9:2)

KH: Hey, Malchus! Are you OK? You seem a little nervous.

Malchus: Well...I don't know if nervous is the right word. I'm certainly confused.

KH: What has you confused?

Malchus: A very zealous young man named Saul of Tarsus just left here with arrest warrants for the people in Damascus who believe in Jesus.

KH: Where are we?

Malchus: This is my boss's house. He is the high priest of Israel.

KH: Is he really authorized to give out arrest warrants?

Malchus: That's a hard question to answer. He does it all the time, but I can't find any Scripture that really grants him authority to do it. It's more of a tradition that no one ever challenged to see if it is legal.

KH: Why does Saul want to arrest people who believe in Jesus? Are these people dangerous or rebellious?

Malchus: That's what has me confused. I don't understand the great hatred both he and my boss have for Jesus and His followers. All the ones I've met are good, law-abiding people. They don't seem to be a threat to anyone. I met Jesus myself one night.

KH: What was He like?

Malchus: He seemed to be the sweetest, kindest, gentlest man I've ever met! My boss, the high priest, had paid one of Jesus' disciples a lot of money to betray Him (Matthew 26:15). The traitor led us to the garden where Jesus was praying. His disciples were sleeping. They were not bothering anyone.

We snuck up on Him to take Him by surprise, but I'm sure He already knew we were coming. It was as if He could read our thoughts (Matthew 9:4; 12:25; Luke 5:22; 6:8)! He just stood there calmly. Everything was going fine until one of our soldiers grabbed Jesus (Matthew 26:50). When he did that, Peter, one of Jesus' disciples, swung a sword at me. I ducked, but he cut off my right ear (Luke 22:50).

KH: Your ear looks fine to me.

Malchus: It is now. That's because Jesus told Peter to put his sword away. Then Jesus picked up my ear and put it back on! It healed instantly and didn't even leave a scar!

We started the fight. We attacked them in the middle of the night while they were praying in a garden doing nothing wrong. Jesus and His disciples had every right to be angry and fight back, but instead, Jesus healed me!

It's as if I can still feel His tender hand on my ear. I've never met a nicer man. He even called the traitor, "Friend" (Matthew 26:50). I've never met a man like Jesus. I don't know why they hate Him so much. It's totally irrational. That's what has me puzzled.

KH: How long has this been going on?

Malchus: Oh, for several years now. It's getting worse. The high priest seemed to hate Jesus long before He even met Him. It's strange. It's much more than just a religious dissagreement. It's almost a demonic hatred!

I had never met Jesus until that night, but I had talked with many people that knew Him. Hundreds had been healed by Him. There was no middle ground. People either loved Him or hated Him. Even those who hated Him couldn't really point to a reason why or to any bad thing He had done. They just hated Him, that's all. It's crazy.

KH: So what do you think is going on?

Malchus: I've worked for the high priest for a long time. He is normally a ice guy, but when the name of Jesus comes up, he goes crazy with hatred. I guess his attitude rubbed off on me for a long time until I actually met Jesus that night and felt His healing touch. There must be money involved. Maybe the priests feel their job is threatened if people follow Jesus.

KH: All evil seems to stem from the love of money (I Timothy 6:10). Say, Malchus, what are you personally going to do about the claims of Jesus? He claimed to be the only way to Heaven, you know.

Malchus: Oh, I know. Don't tell my boss but...I believe Jesus was right.

KH: When your boss had Jesus crucified, did it satisfy his anger?

Malchus: Yes, for a few days. He was giddy with joy. But then, rumors started flying that Jesus had risen from the dead. My boss was scared and angry. He gave a lot of money to the soldiers to spread the rumor that Jesus' body was stolen by His disciples (Matthew 28:11-13). We all know this was a lie because Roman law requires the soldiers to be killed if they fail at their job and those soldiers are still alive.

Jesus appeared to hundreds of people (Acts 1:3; I Corinthians 15:4-8). Now there are many thousands of believers. The high priest is frantic to stop the spread of this new religion! That's why Saul got the warrants.

KH: Why doesn't he honestly examine the evidence and accept Jesus as the Messiah?

Malchus: That's what I did. I've been secretly attending the meetings of the disciples. I need to keep it quiet for now. If my boss found out, I'd be fired...or worse!

KH: What about this guy who just left?

Malchus: Let's pray for him. "Dear Heavenly Father, Please stop Saul from persecuting Your children. Please convert him, Lord. Do whatever You need to do to get his attention, Lord. In Jesus name, Amen."

KH: Amen. Thanks, Malchus.

Malchus: You are welcome, Kent.

See Acts 9:3-20 for the rest of the story!

OH, NO!, NOW WHAT?
November 13th 2007
(based on Acts 28:30)

GOD: Good morning, Son!

KH: God! It's 4:15 in the morning! Don't You ever get tired?

GOD: No, Son. I never slumber or sleep (Psalm 121:3-4).

KH: Well, I do! What could You possibly want at this hour that can't wait till morning?

GOD: It is morning, Son.

KH: Maybe in England, but not here!

GOD: You prayed last night and asked Me to guide you and talk to you. That's why I'm here. You asked Me to help you make it through this time of great testing for you, your family, and the creation ministry I led you to start nearly twenty years ago, didn't you?

KH: Yes, Lord, I did.

GOD: That's what I'm here for, Son. When I see you are nearly maxed out, I take some heat off and send relief to help seal the lessons learned into your mind and soul.

KH: What have I learned, Lord?

GOD: I don't lead My children to trials and tribulation; I lead them through them. Do another "All Call" with knee-mail. They will explain it.

KH: OK, Lord. All Call! Is anyone up this early and willing to explain how God helped you through your trials and tests?

Noah: I'm up and would be glad to help! God helped me hundreds of times but I'll only tell you about three of those times.

1. *He helped me make it through a time when all of society was wicked. Nobody wanted to serve God (Genesis 6:8, 12; 7:1). I asked God to help me raise godly sons in a vile world and He did!*
2. *I made it through all the scoffing as I did what God said and built the ark. The ridicule was incredible...until the rain started. Don't listen to the scoffers. They can't swim long enough to steal your joy! Keep building!*
3. *I made it through the year on the ark during the Flood. I felt confined, because I was. But God used that year to change the world—literally! I know you are confined right now, Kent, but there will be a whole new world for you when you get out. Relax, go for a cruise.*

Why On Earth Did God Let This Happen... For Heaven's Sake?

Joseph: Hey, Kent. God brought me through my prison time in Egypt and really opened doors for me to save the world because of it (Genesis 45:4-8)! The brothers that mocked me and hated me later came begging for me to provide for them (Genesis 42:6). God will bring you through. Even some that mock and hate you now will come to God.

KH: Thanks, guys!

Job: Hey, Kent. I didn't ask for trouble but it came anyway (Job 1-2)! I cried a lot, but God brought me through and gave me double! He knows what He is doing. It's OK to cry, complain, and throw dust, but don't quit!

KH: Thanks, Job. I can't wait to see you in Heaven.

Job: You won't believe this place! It will be worth it all! Go through the trial—you will come forth as gold (Job 23:10).

Job's Oldest Son: Hey, Kent, all nine of my siblings were eating at my house when the storm blew in from nowhere. We were all crushed as the house collapsed (Job 1:19). As I was trapped and bleeding to death, I said, "Why God?" God replied, "Trust Me. You will know why in a few minutes." Boy! Was He right! All ten of us died that day but now that we've been here for four thousand years, we know it is because......[Sorry, message blocked by knee-mail. Just have faith, Son.]

Abraham: I made it through, Kent. I went through years of questioning why my wife and I had no children. My brother, Nahor, had twelve children (Genesis 22:20-24)! My wife and I cried at every family reunion for years. Wow! That was hard! But once it was over and Isaac was born—Wow! What joy (Genesis 21:6-7)! We all sing a song up here in Heaven. It's called, "It's over now!" We are all watching you and cheering for you, Kent. Hang in there! You'll be able to join our choir one day.

KH: Thanks, Abraham. Will I be able to sing it without crying? I can't down here.

Abraham: Probably not. God is so awesome! I wish I hadn't doubted Him that time when I got Hagar.

KH: We all agree, Abraham. That three dollars per gallon at the gas pump is a constant reminder.

Abraham: Sorry about that. But hey, lots of Ishmael's kids are up here, too. They are cheering as well.

Moses: Oh, Kent, where do I start? God saw me through so much! I was raised in a heathen environment by an Egyptian step-mom. I killed a man and became a fugitive from the law for forty years. It's hard to sleep when every sound you hear could be the Egyptian police coming to get you! God saw me through it all.

He saw me through the hard time with hard-hearted Pharaoh at the Red Sea (Exodus 14:13-31); through forty years of wandering in the Wilderness trusting God for food and water every day. He was faithful. He saw me through it all. He will with you, too.

Joshua: Hey, Kent! I was real discouraged when ten of my fellow spies voted not to obey God (Numbers 13-14). They even wanted to stone me for suggesting we do right (Numbers 14:6-10)! Their sin cost me forty years of my life! I had to wander in the desert until they all died (Numbers 14:30-34; Deuteronomy 1:38). It's discouraging knowing you must suffer due to other's sins.

KH: I know about that one.

Joshua: But when God worked a miracle for us to cross the flooded Jordan (Joshua 3-4), I forgot all the wasted years! For years afterward, I would cry for joy every time I saw that pile of rocks we left to remind us of God's provision (Joshua 4:4-7). He brought us through Jordan, through the walls of Jericho (Joshua 6), and through nearly all of our enemies. The children of Israel were not faithful to finish the job in defeating the enemies (Judges 1). God was faithful though. Keep following Him, Kent, and finish the job of defeating every sin in your life.

KH: Thanks, Joshua. I'll work on that. So far it's been almost thirty-nine years of battles and I'm still not able to conquer several of the giants I face.

Joshua: Just keep fighting sin until you die, then.

KH: OK. I'll try.

Daniel: I made it through, Kent. I admit it was real scary going in the den of lions and scary, smelly, and uncomfortable while I was in there; but it's over now (Daniel 6:16, 26, 27). Looking back I can say, "Thanks, God! That was cool!" Pray even if your situation makes no sense to you.

KH: Thanks, Daniel.

Shadrach: My two friends and I made it through the furnace, Kent (Daniel 3)!

KH: Were you scared?

Shadrach: Hey, we are human! Of course we were scared! The king was real angry! It's never a good idea to make a powerful politician angry because you won't bow to his ego. Once they decide to fry you, they know how to make it seven times hotter (Daniel 3:19)! Since we had obeyed God and tried to please Him, He stepped in—

literally! When God stepped into that furnace, everything was fine (Daniel 3:25)! We didn't even feel the heat. It burned off our bands and we were able to change the minds and hearts of an entire nation (Daniel 3:28-30). Untold thousands believed in God and were saved because we stayed true and let God bring us through the test, not save us from the test. All the Babylonian converts from that special fire Sunday service are up here cheering for you, Kent (Hebrews 12:1). Don't bend, don't bow, and you won't burn. Keep running.

KH: Thanks, guys. I love your stories!

Isaac: Hey, Kent, I made it. I knew God had promised my dad, Abraham, that I would have children (Genesis 21:12), yet Dad was asking me to lie down on an altar so he could kill me (Genesis 22:9)! I was a teenager and Dad was one hundred years older than I was. I could have easily refused and run away from him, but I trusted God to keep His promise. It was pretty tense there for a while, but God brought both Dad and me through the trial of our faith. God seems to like waiting until the last minute.

KH: Boy! That's for sure!

Isaac: You will be fine, Kent. God never fails.

Golden Candlestick: Hey, Kent, you should see all that I went through (Exodus 25:31-37)! First, I was dug out of the ground, heated in a furnace until all the impurities were gone, then beaten on for many days until I was in the desired shape. I made it through all of that and was able to stand for centuries in the tabernacle and later the temple. God brought me through so He could use me for His glory! It was worth it all!

GOD: That's enough for now. My Word is full of examples where I brought people to a trial so that I could bring them through it. It's all part of a much bigger plan that your little brain won't hold. Trust Me.

KH: I do trust You, Lord. I just want to go home!

GOD: I've got it all under control, Son. You are not there just for you. I'm doing a work in many lives in and out of the prison through this trying time for you. Hold My hand and relax. I'll get you through. I've got your back.

A SOLDIER - FOR THE DURATION
November 15th 2007

GOD: Good morning, Son! Come with Me and listen to this conversation.

Red: (Red is a twenty-one-year-old in Pittsburgh, PA in 1941. Everyone calls him "Red" because of his red hair and freckles.)

Hey, Mom, I joined the Marines!

Mom: Oh, Son! I don't know how to feel about that. Your father died two years ago. Your older sister got married. It's just you and I, Son. Times are so hard now. I need you here to help out.

Red: But Mom, the Japs bombed Pearl Harbor last week! The President is calling for volunteers to join the war effort. I've got to go!

Mom: Son, you are only twenty-one. Your whole life is ahead of you. You could be killed or wounded. Then what would I do?

Red: Mom, if I don't go, they may come to attack us here. I've got to go to protect you, Sis, and our country. We didn't start this fight but we've been attacked. There is no other choice now. We must fight to defend ourselves.

Mom: Oh, Son, there will be plenty of other young men who join up. You could stay here and work in a steel mill to supply equipment for the war.

Red: Mom, you know I love you and wouldn't hurt you for the world, but this is something I have got to do! I leave in three weeks.

Mom: How long did you enlist for, two years?

Red: For the duration of the war.

Mom: What does that mean?

Red: I'll be fighting until it's over. It's them or us.

Mom: Oh, Son! You are a man now. You can make your own decisions. This rips my heart out, but I love you and I'm proud of you!

Red: I'll write you every chance I get and send you as much of my pay as I can to help out here. You will make it, Mom. I'll be back. I promise.

Mom: Son, you realize that enlisting means that you are giving your mind, body, and future to Uncle Sam, don't you? You must obey every command he gives, even if it means your death.

Red: I know, Mom. I'm dedicating everything to this cause.

Mom: Son, let's pray for God to protect you and give us the victory.

Three Weeks Later

Officer: Next! OK, Soldier: name, height, weight, and shoe size!

Red: Robert B. Hovind, sir, six foot two, two hundred twenty pounds, size twelve shoe, sir.

KH: Oh, God! Thank you for protecting my dad for those four awful years! He dedicated everything for the cause of freedom. He saw all twenty-five of his fellow classmates in training get killed! Those Marines gave it all!

GOD: Yes, Son, war is awful, and those Marines were dedicated.

KH: Lord....I know there is a great war going on for the minds and souls of men.

GOD: Yes, there is, Son, ever since the Garden of Eden.

KH: Lord....I don't have much to offer, but You can have me. I'm Yours to use however You want and whenever You want, even in prison........for the duration.

GOD: I accept your offer, Son,—again.

KH: Lord...I signed up the first time almost thirty-nine years ago now. Does boot camp ever end?

GOD: Well, boot camp ends, but I often call My soldiers to get further training for new assignments. I'll re-assign you soon, Son. Go back to sleep. Training continues when you wake up. I've got your back.

GADDI - DISOBEDIENCE, DISTRUST, ANGER AND MURDER
November 16th 2007

(based on Numbers 13:11-14 and Numbers 38)

KH: Excuse me, Mr. Gaddi, what is going on?

Gaddi: I'm looking for some good rocks to stone somebody with.

KH: Why?

Gaddi: Moses and Aaron lied to us! Then Joshua and Caleb voted against us.

KH: What did Moses and Aaron lie about?

Gaddi: They came to Egypt about two years ago and said God had sent them to deliver all of us Hebrews out of slavery and bring us into a "promised land that flows with milk and honey" (Numbers 13:27). Ha! What a lie!

I just got back from searching that "promised land" for forty days. It flows with milk and honey all right, but it would also flow with our blood if we tried to go in there. We could never defeat the giants that live there.

KH: Aren't you a descendent of Joseph, the great leader in Egypt (Numbers 13:11)?

Gaddi: Yes, I am.

KH: Weren't you chosen to be one of the twelve to search out the land because you were already a leader in your tribe and they trusted you (Numbers 13:2)?

Gaddi: Yes, I was.

KH: Were you there in Egypt to see all ten of the plagues God brought on Pharoah and Egypt?

Gaddi: Yes, I saw them all.

KH: Wasn't Pharaoh the most powerful ruler of the world's most powerful nation when God made him let you all go free?

Gaddi: Yes, he was.

KH: Didn't you see God part the Red Sea and then drown Pharaoh and his army?

Gaddi: Yes, I did.

KH: Didn't you see God bring water out of a rock (Exodus 1:7), bread and flesh from the sky (Exodus 16), and protection from the Amalekites with a stick (Exodus 17:8-13)?

Gaddi: Yes, I saw it all.

KH: Did you hear God speak from the mountain and promise to obey Him (Exodus 19:7-8)?

Gaddi: Yes, I did.

KH: Didn't God tell Moses that He was giving the land to the children of Israel (Number 13:2)?

Gaddi: Yes, He did.

KH: Then why don't you trust and obey and take the land?

Gaddi: I'm scared! We can't conquer that land. There are giants that live there. All the people are huge (Numbers 13:28-33)! I've got to stone Moses to stop this mass suicide.

KH: Well, Gaddi... let me give you my opinion. First, I think that being scared is normal, fine, and even wise most of the time. Second, I think you are exaggerating, slandering, and lying. All the people are not giants, are they (Numbers 13:32)?

Gaddi: Well… no. But some are!

KH: Do you really think it would be better to go back to slavery in Egypt (Numbers 14:3)?

Gaddi: Better a live slave than a dead Hebrew.

KH: Those aren't the only two options. You left out "live a free man!" Third, you are spreading your fear to others and encouraging them to disobey God. You are sowing discord among the brethren. God hates this (Proverbs 6:19).

Fourth, you have gone beyond sowing discord to encouraging open rebellion (I Samuel 15:23; Jeremiah 28:16) against God's plan and God's man (Numbers 14:2, 4, 36; Psalm 105:15).

Fifth, you harbor hatred in your heart (Psalm 66:18) for godly men like Moses, Aaron, Joshua, and Caleb because their faith makes your cowardice look bad.

Sixth, you have gone beyond hatred to consider and encourage murder of God's men (Numbers 14:10) to cover your sin!

I think God is angry with you, Gaddi. He gave you leadership skills and position and you have used it for evil. Leaders are judged more harshly than others (James 3:1). I think your decision today will cause two million people to experience much misery and many wasted years (Numbers 14:23-30). You will die today, Gaddi (Numbers 14:37-40).

Gaddi: Move over, Kent. I've found my rocks, and here comes Moses now....

KH: Some people will not listen.

ZIMRI AND COZBI - ADULTERY
November 13th 2007
(based on Numbers 25:3-18)

KH: (At Numbers 25:6) Whoa there, folks! What are you doing dressed like that?! Put some clothes on!

Zimri: We are going to walk slowly right past old pious Moses, the judges, and the whole congregation of Israel right into my tent to make love.

I'm tired of all those silly moral laws Moses tries to put on us (Exodus 20:14). He doesn't want us to enjoy life. We will show those do-gooders what they are missing out on. They are a bunch of old fogies way out of touch with the times.

KH: But Cozbi, aren't you embarrassed to be outside in broad daylight dressed like that? It looks like you were poured into those jeans and they forgot to say, "When!"

Cozbi: Oh, no! I like my clothes tight, low cut, and see through—to show off all my curves. I get a lot of attention from the men dressed like this.

KH: I'm sure you do, but my daddy always said, "If you're not in business, don't advertise!"

Cozbi: But I am in business!

KH: You two aren't married, are you?

Cozbi: Of course we are! Just not to each other. My husband is off with another woman and Zimri's wife is probably off "praying" for him. She doesn't understand him like I do.

KH: But Zimri, didn't you hear God give the Ten Commandments to Moses, including the one about not committing adultery?

Zimri: No, that was my dad almost forty years ago. I was not born yet. Dad tried to tell me about it, but I wasn't interested in that church stuff. Plus, Dad was always too busy trying to get ahead in politics. He's a prince, you know (Numbers 25:14). He never had much time to teach me about life; so I learned from my friends (Proverbs 7:7). I'll be able to be a prince also one day. My dad has connections.

KH: I know. That means many others will look to you for leadership. I don't think what you are doing today is setting a good example for the young boys around you to follow, is it?

Zimri: I'm more concerned about me right now. Besides, why would God care what I do as long as it doesn't hurt anybody? Plus, it's not like I'm the only one. There are twenty-four thousand of us that have Midianite girlfriends (Numbers 25:9; I Corinthians 10:8). Get with the times, Kent, everyone is doing it.

Cozbi: Yeah, Kent, it's not like we are complete heathens. We came from Abraham, too, and we worship god (Genesis 25:2). We just call him Baal. Our god doesn't have strict rules like Moses. Our god encourages adultery. On top of that, Zimri and I are both children of important political leaders. The rules for the common folk don't apply to us.

KH: I think God will judge everyone by the same standard. He is not impressed with politics, power, or titles.

Cozbi: Well, we just do things differently in my country. If you feel it's right for you, then it's OK. I know men and how they think and react. I'm real good at putting that knowledge to work.

KH: Do you know or care how God thinks or reacts?

Cozbi: Not really.

KH: Zimri, you know this girl was raised in a pretty heathen world without knowledge of the true God. She has not seen God provide manna from Heaven like you have (Exodus 16:15-35; Deuteronomy 8:16; John 6:31-58). She didn't see God do any miracles (Numbers 16:31; 17:8). She has not been able to read or hear the great laws God gave to your people. She needs to be converted, Zimri. Aren't you concerned about her soul?

Zimri: Not really.

KH: What about the effect your actions will have on your wife and children?

Zimri: I don't really care. It's not important to me.

KH: What if it's important to God?

Zimri & Cozbi: Look, we don't care and we are kind of in a hurry right now. We want to see Moses' reaction when we walk past.

KH: Oh, you will get a reaction, all right! Phinehas will help both of you get the point (Numbers 25:7).

COLONEL SANFORD - WHY?
November 26th 2007

GOD: Good morning, Son!

KH: Good morning, Lord. Thanks for a new day. Thanks also just for being God. You keep every atom in the universe together even though the positive protons should repel each other. How do you keep everything from exploding?

GOD: That's My secret, Son (Colossians 1:16-17). I'll show you one day.

KH: Thanks also for giving me time to read so much this last year. I was so busy (like Martha), traveling and preaching for seventeen years that I got behind on reading all the good books out there. They are changing me in a thousand ways.

GOD: You are welcome, Son. You've read a lot, but there are many more that will help you grow even more.

KH: I know, Lord. Can I read them at home instead of here?

GOD: Yes, Son, soon.

KH: Thanks for letting me find this book, Trail of Tears - The Rise and Fall of the Cherokee Nation written by John Ehle and published by Anchor Books, Doubleday in New York in 1988. I had read some about what happened to the Cherokee Indians, but wow! This story is tearing my heart out! How could people be so cruel to their fellow man?

GOD: It's always the same reason, Son—the love of money (I Timothy 6:10). You see, ever since I cursed the ground (Genesis 3:17) and required that everyone must work for their own good, people have sought for ways to get around this. They want others to work and then they will steal or cheat them out of the fruit of their labor. Read I Timothy 6:10 carefully, Son. All evil, including what happened to the Cherokees, can be traced back to the love of money.

KH: Why do you allow all the evil, Lord?

GOD: I don't, Son.

KH: How can You say that? I'm surrounded by suffering and evil. Billions of evil acts are done every day and the evildoer gets by with it.

GOD: No they don't, Son. Let me explain it like Abraham did one time (Genesis 18:24-32). Suppose every time a sin is committed, I judge it ten minutes later. Would that be justice?

KH: Yes, Lord, swift justice.

GOD: What if I waited twenty minutes to judge the evil, to give them time to repent and judge themselves (I Corinthians 11:31)? Would that still be justice?

KH: Yes, Lord. I see where You are going. What if You waited twenty years or two hundred years? You would still be just. You really don't allow any sin to go unpunished, do You?

GOD: No, Son. I see them all and judge them all. Everyone faces Me after death for judgment (Hebrews 9:27). I keep careful records, Son (Matthew 12:36). Just because I don't execute sentence against an evil work right away (Ecclesiastes 8:11) doesn't mean I won't.

KH: Lord, how could Colonel Sanford of the Georgia Guard sleep at night after what he did to the missionaries who were reaching out to the Cherokees (Trail of Tears, pp. 244-247)?

GOD: Ask him, Son.

KH: OK. Excuse me, Colonel Sanford, what is going on here?

Colonel Sanford (CS): I'm just doing my sworn duty, Kent. I'm taking this criminal in to join the others for trial.

KH: Isn't that "criminal" Mr. Worcester, the long-term missionary to the Cherokees? Why do you call him a criminal?

CS: Yes, that's Mr. Worcester. I call him a criminal because assigning him a negative label makes it easier for me to sleep at night. If I said I was arresting a "missionary" or a "man of God" or even a "man," it would make it hard. Labels are important. We are taught that in our training for this job. It's OK to arrest criminals, isn't it?

KH: Yes, labels help sooth the conscience. Hitler did that with labels like "Jews" or "subhumans" or "leaches."

CS: Who?

KH: Never mind. I see some things never change. There are lots of labels like "terrorist" or "felon" or "religious wacko" that people use for the same reasons today.

Since he has not been tried yet, isn't he innocent until proven guilty? Even then, possibly innocent during appeal, and maybe even innocent regardless of what the court system says?

CS: Technically yes, but I work for Governor Gilmer of the state of Georgia, and our state passed a law that all white men in Georgia must get a license to live on Cherokee lands. These criminals don't have one, so I'm arresting them.

KH: I'm sure you know there is still a question about whether Georgia law applies on Cherokee lands, don't you?

CS: I don't get into politics. I'm a soldier just doing my job.

KH: Didn't you take an oath to defend the constitution?

CS: Yes.

KH: Didn't you arrest this same man two years ago?

CS: Yes, I did.

KH: Did you have a warrant from a judge or magistrate to do that?

CS: No, but I had an order from my boss; so I did it. I've got to keep my job to feed my family.

KH: Ah, yes....I Timothy 6:10. When you arrested him, why did you wait until night, bring twenty-five men, and surround the house with guns and bayonets? You knew they were peaceful people who had been missionaries for years. You also knew there were women and children inside, didn't you?

CS: We use excessive force to instill terror. We find it makes people respect and fear us. We love to see people cower and tremble when we approach. It's an ego thing. It gives us a feeling of power. You would have to experience it to understand. This criminal has been writing articles in the newspaper that are critical of the way Georgia is treating the Indians.

KH: Isn't that what freedom of speech and the press is all about?

CS: Don't get smart with me, Kent, or I'll arrest you, too!

KH: When you arrested him two years ago, you knew he was also the federal postmaster in the town, didn't you?

CS: Yes, and that's how he got out of being tried, but Governor Gilmer made sure he lost that job; so this time, he will have to get a license or move out. The governor told me to deliver the letter with his options.

KH: Since the issue of ownership of Cherokee lands is still not settled, why doesn't Governor Gilmer wait until it is?

CS: Georgia laid claim to their land and Georgia is going to show President Jackson a thing or two about state's rights, that's why. We want that land. It's worth a fortune!

KH: Ah...I Timothy 6:10 again. When you delivered the letter to the missionaries, why did you add the part about having ten days to move out? That wasn't from the governor, was it?

CS: No, but I thought it added to my authority. See this insignia? I'm a colonel! People obey me.

KH: Why are you making them wear chains and walk the whole thirty miles while you all ride? They offered to provide their own horses.

CS: We are taller on the horses, which adds to our ego. Plus, there is nothing like a thirty-mile hike carrying chains to make people tired, hungry, and submissive to authority.

KH: Why didn't you let them say good-bye to their wives and children? You must know that it terrorized them as well.

CS: Adding family stress helps bring the criminals into submission as well. That's what we are taught in our training.

KH: Doesn't hearing the cries of the women and children make it hard for you to sleep at night?

CS: I don't let myself think about it. I'm just doing my job arresting criminals. I've got to do my job to feed my family, you know.

KH: Ah...I Timothy 6:10 again. I think I'm seeing a pattern here. Does knowing that these men will spend four years in prison at hard labor away from their families and ministry bother you?

CS: Look, Kent, I told you, I'm just doing my job.

KH: God, did You see it all?

GOD: Yes, Son, I saw it all and took care of it. You will see when you get up here. Keep reading, praying, and winning souls. Everyone is in trouble on judgment day unless they have accepted My free gift (Romans 6:23). Keep warning them, Son (James 5:20). I've got your back.

KENT AND THE SCIENTIST ON THE LIVING WORD
November 28th 2007

GOD: Good morning, Son. I heard your prayers. Hold My hand. I want to show you something.

KH: OK. Where are we, Lord? What year is it? Who is this man?

GOD: It doesn't matter, Son. Talk to him.

KH: Excuse me, sir, you look a little puzzled. Why are you weighing this tree?

Scientist (SC): I can't figure it out. Where did the tree come from?

KH: Ah...trees come from seeds.

SC: I know that, but it doesn't make sense. Five years ago I cut this oak barrel in half and filled it with dirt until it weighed exactly 200 pounds. Then I put a seed in the dirt and watered it every day. Each fall I put the dead leaves back on the dirt.

Today I pulled out the tree, roots and all and brushed the dirt off into the barrel and weighed both. The tree weighs just over 200 pounds and the dirt still weighs 199 pounds 14 ounces. That is only 2 ounces less than five years ago!

KH: That's interesting!

SC: That's why I'm puzzled. Where did the tree come from? All I added was water for five years.

KH: Yes, quite a puzzle. Any answers?

SC: I don't know. It was still growing when I pulled it out. It would have been 500 pounds or more if I had waited.

GOD: OK, Son. Let's go home.

KH: Wow, Lord! Wow! Where did the tree come from?

GOD: This lesson is for you, Son. The seed knows how to make the tree. It doesn't need much from the dirt. You just add water, sun, and air, and be patient.

You received Me into your life on February 9, 1969, didn't you, Son (John 1:12; 3:3-7)?

KH: Yes, Lord. I did.

GOD: I'm like the seed and you are like the dirt. I am growing a whole new person in you (II Corinthians 5:17; Ephesians 4:15; Hebrews 5:13-14; I Peter 2:2; II Peter 3:18). Just add water and you will grow.

Trees can't run from the heat, Son. Neither can you. A big tree will easily use over one hundred gallons of water each day. The hotter it is, the more they need. They send roots down until they can get enough. People who work or run in the heat need lots of water, too.

KH: Thanks, Lord! I needed that. I was feeling the heat of my situation and asked You to help me stand the heat (II Corinthians 12:7-10). That's my answer, isn't it, Lord?

GOD: Yes, Son. Just keep adding water. This present trial is to help you put roots deeper into My Word. You will find all you need. The Living Water (John 4:13-14) that I give will let you stand the worst heat that man can provide (Daniel 3:19-25).

KH: How will I know when I've taken in enough water?

GOD: You won't feel the heat (Daniel 3:25). Chill out, Son. I've got your back.

ONE MORE NIGHT WITH THE FROGS
November 29th 2007
(based on Exodus 8:1-14)

(At Exodus 8:10)

KH: Excuse me, Mr. Pharoah, sir, why are there frogs everywhere? Who is that old man walking out the door? Why do you have that smirk on your face?

Pharoah (PH): Ha! I showed him!

KH: Showed who?

PH: That old man walking out the door. That's Moses.

KH: What did you show him?

PH: I showed him who's boss, that's what!

KH: How did you do that?

PH: With the frogs, man, the frogs!

KH: I don't understand. Do you like having your palace full of frogs like this?

PH: No! Of course, not! I hate them! They are in my royal bedroom, in the oven, in the bread machine, everywhere! There are millions of them. I hate them!

KH: I still don't get it. How do these frogs show Moses?

PH: That guy Moses came in here last week claiming some God of his told him that I was supposed to release all my slaves. Yeah right! I've got things to build around here. I'm not about to let them go.

Then Moses did a few magic tricks but I was not impressed. I still wouldn't let them go. So, yesterday, he called for a plague of frogs, and here they are.

KH: I see that. So how does that show Moses that you are the boss? I don't understand.

PH: Well, you see, it didn't take me long to realize these frogs would be a real problem; so I called for Moses to take them away and he agreed to do it.

KH: But they are still here.

PH: That's how I showed him! He asked me when I wanted them to be taken away and I said, "Tomorrow." That showed him.

KH: Showed him what?

PH: That I'm the boss! Don't you see? Moses knows my wives hate frogs in their socks and that they make the bread taste funny. He also knows I want them gone so he expected me to beg him to get rid of them today. Ha! Not me! I'm Pharoah! I said, "Tomorrow!" just to show him.

KH: Ah....do you really want to spend one more night with the frogs?

PH: Not really, but I have to maintain my image. Do you think it worked? You saw him walk out. Was he impressed?

KH: Oh....I'd say you made an impression all right! He's probably out there telling people about you right now.

PH: Oh, good! It's hard to be Pharoah, but someone has to do it. Hey, Kent, get this frog out of my hair, would you?

KH: Sure. I think you are in for a long night. Maybe your musicians could write a song about this.

PH: Great idea! We'll call it, "One More Night with the Frogs. That'll show 'em." Do you think it will sell?

KH: I'll buy one.

PH: Thanks, Kent, you're a true friend.

KH: Ah....You are welcome.

WHAT A GIFT!
December 1st 2007

GOD: See, Son. I told you I would provide (Philippians 4:19).

KH: I see that, Lord. I'm so sorry for doubting and complaining. When I saw the copy of that check I cried. How humbling! How can one woman in Virginia give so much to help support our ministry? It's incredible, Lord! Thanks!

GOD: Tell Dan about it, Son.

KH: Hey, Dan! Remember when we prayed a few days ago for God to provide the needs of Creation Science Evangelism while I'm locked up?

Dan: Yes, I remember.

KH: Well...here is proof that God heard and answered that prayer! Look at this check Marie sent to support CSE!

Dan: Wow, $1.94!

KH: Look at the memo line.

Dan: Wow! "The widow's mite." That's awesome!

KH: In the last eighteen years of ministry, we've had lots of people donate to support our gospel outreach, but I can't remember ever getting a gift that encouraged me like this one! Praise God! We will make it through this trial. With supporters like this, there is no need that God cannot meet.

Dan: I agree. That's awesome! Thanks for showing me.

KH: God, please bless Marie more than she can stand.

GOD: Oh, I will, Son, I will. Go get supper, Son. I've got your back.

FOUR HUNDRED DAYS
December 7th 2007

KH: Ah...Lord? Today is my four hundredth day in prison. That's 9,600 hours or 576,000 minutes of being locked up.

GOD: I know, Son. I've been with you the entire 34,560,000 seconds. Did you have a question, Son?

KH: Well...ah...yes, Lord. Are You still watching my case?

GOD: Oh, yes, Son, very closely. Many people are. I'm on top of things. Any more questions?

KH: Well...ah...yes, Lord. When will it be over?

GOD: Now, Son, you have known Me for over 14,000 days. You know I won't tell you that. Do you trust Me?

KH: I'm trying, Lord. It's hard because there are so many things about this that I don't understand and certainly some things I don't like as well.

I've read a lot of books, learned a lot of things, and hopefully, brought many people to You during this time, but I'd rather be back out preaching. There are still billions of people who need to hear about You; plus, I really miss my family and freedom.

GOD: Now, Son, I was concerned about lost souls long before you were ever born (II Peter 3:9). I have lots of My children working on that problem. Plus, you are still reaching people. Your son and staff are continuing the ministry. Your bonds have motivated many to start ministries (Philippians 1:14) and the DVDs still reach people every day. You read the letters last night that I had sent in, didn't you?

KH: Yes, Lord. Thank You! It is so encouraging to get mail from people who are excited about getting saved after watching the videos!

GOD: As for missing your family and freedom, Son, I understand. When you are done with this special assignment I have You on, I'll repay double like I did with Job (Job 42:10). Right now, there are some people I am using you to reach for My kingdom there.

KH: Can I at least get a glimpse of the mission today, Lord?

GOD: All right, Son. Pay close attention as you preach in the Spanish church tonight. You will see the tip of the tip of the iceberg.

9:30 p.m…

KH: Wow, Lord! Wow! I never dreamed [name edited by knee-mail] would come to the service! He has always been pretty profane and showed little interest in spiritual things. He stayed and asked questions for an hour and a half! You have been working on him for a long time, haven't You, Lord?

GOD: Yes, Son. You are part of My plan to reach him. He's been watching you like a hawk, but you are too oblivious to know it. He has been talking about you to lots of staff and inmates. By My grace, they have seen you go through these trials and keep a smile on your face.

They are really under conviction, Son. Especially [name blocked by knee-mail]. He has seen many who claim to be Christians come and go over the years, but quite a few have not maintained a good testimony. He wants what you have, Son. I know this has been a long trial for you, but be patient. It's working.

KH: Thanks, Lord. I asked You to give me a glimpse today and You sure did. Lord, would You please give me another glimpse tomorrow and every day from now on? It sure makes this trial easier to bear.

GOD: That's a reasonable request, Son. I promise to make Myself known to you every day.

MICHAL, SAUL'S DAUGHTER
December 18th 2007

KH: Excuse me, ma'am. Why are you eating in here all by yourself and crying? This palace is full of kids running everywhere full of joy and laughter. Why do you look so sad?

Michal: Oh...that's a long, sad story. It's depressing. My family was pretty dysfunctional. I doubt you'd want to hear about it.

KH: Yes, I would, if you don't mind telling it.

Michal: OK. I was the youngest of five children (I Samuel 14:49). I had three older brothers and an older sister. My dad was Saul, the first king of Israel. He was real tall (I Samuel 9:2) but real shy and humble when he was first made king (I Samuel 10:21-22). The longer he was king, the more proud and independent he became.

KH: Did he love the Lord?

Michal: That's a tough question. There were times when he did (I Samuel 9:25; 10:6-13; 15:24-30) and other times when he acted like a heathen (I Samuel 16:14; 18:9-12). Some days he was humble and other days he was full of pride. Some days he obeyed God and other times he did not (I Samuel 15). It was hard for us five kids to know what kind of mood he would be in from day to day.

KH: Is that why you live in the palace, because your dad is king?

Michal: No. My dad was king, but he was jealous of David, the young man who killed Goliath (I Samuel 17:49-51). Dad had said he would give my sister, Merab, to the one who killed Goliath (I Samuel 17:25; 18:17-19) but he went back on that promise. I fell in love with David the first time I saw him (I Samuel 18:20) and when Dad found out, he decided to try to use me to get David killed by the Philistines (I Samuel 18:21, 25). He said if David killed one hundred Philistines, he could marry me.

KH: Did David really kill one hundred Philistines?

Michal: Oh, no. To show his love for me, he killed two hundred of them (I Samuel 18:27)! We were very happily married for a while (I Samuel 18:28). David was such a godly man. It was easy for me to love him. My brother, Jonathan, also loved David (I Samuel 18:3; 19:2) and when Dad plotted to kill David, we helped him escape (I Samuel 19). When Dad's paid assassins came, I lied to them to give David time to escape. David went and spent time with the great prophet Samuel (I Samuel 19:18) and then fled again into hiding for several years (I Samuel 20-25). Dad made me marry Phalti since David was gone (I Samuel 25:44).

KH: What did David think of that?

Michal: He was heartbroken, but with Dad and the army chasing him as he was running for his life, there was nothing either of us could do. He married two other women (I Samuel 25:42-43) and I was called on to raise my five nephews, the sons of my sister Merab and her husband Adriel (I Samuel 18:19; II Samuel 21:8).

When Dad died (I Samuel 31:4) and my half brother became king, (II Samuel 2:8-9), things were pretty unstable for a while with two kings over different parts of the country (II Samuel 2:8-3:11). After a few years, Abner, my brother's head general, offered to meet with David to try to bring the whole kingdom together under one king—David.

David said he would not meet with him unless he brought me with him (II Samuel 3:13). I thought it was pretty cool that David still loved me after all those years and wanted me back.

KH: What did your husband think?

Michal: Oh, he was upset about losing me, but not enough to really fight for me. He gave up pretty easily (II Samuel 3:14-16).

KH: How was it getting back with David after all those years?

Michal: I expected it to be like it was when we first got married, but I was now his seventh wife and never felt special like I did before. Later some evil men murdered my brother, the king (II Samuel 4:1-8) and David became king of all Israel (II Samuel 5:1-10). He married even more women (II Samuel 5:13) and I felt left out even more.

KH: I don't really understand your culture, but didn't God say that the king should not have more than one wife (Deuteronomy 17:17)?

Michal: Yes, He did, but all the kings around us had many wives, so David tried to be like all of them. It sure causes lots of family problems that way. The king has many children but he can't really spend quality time with them; so they are pretty much raised by the mothers.

KH: OK. That explains why you are living in the palace as one of David's wives, but I still don't understand why you are eating by yourself and crying.

Michal: Well, when my husband David was bringing the ark of God back to Jerusalem, he was so happy (II Samuel 6:14). He was dancing around naked in public and didn't care (II Samuel 6:20). I saw him out the window and lost respect for him. I actually began to despise him in my heart (II Samuel 6:14; I Chronicles 15:29).

KH: I think you are exaggerating. He wasn't really naked, was he (II Samuel 6:14)?

Michal: Well...practically naked. He had taken off his royal robe and just had the ephod on.

KH: Michal, the linen ephod was designed by God and is really modest (Exodus 20, 28). I think that your tendency to exaggerate the negative shows a deeper problem of the heart and will strain any marriage. Was the problem his dancing and praising God or was it really a bad attitude in your heart? I think you may have lost your first love (Revelation 2:4).

Michal: I see what you mean. I guess going from being his one-and-only love to being a small part of a big kingdom has caused me to get bitter (Hebrews 12:15). I never saw it growing in me.

KH: Has anything else helped to rob your joy and to make you bitter?

Michal: I'd have to give you a little history to explain it, but...yes.

KH: That's fine. I love history.

Michal: Well, when Joshua led the people of Israel to conquer this land four hundred years ago, the Gibeonites fooled him into making a league with them (Joshua 9). The Gibeonites should have all been killed by God's command, but Joshua's treaty saved their lives. My dad couldn't stand them; and when he became king, he killed lots of them. Dad never cared much for following God's laws very closely. Anyway, God sent a famine on Israel and David asked God why (II Samuel 21:1). God told him it was because of what my dad had done to the Gibeonites; so David called in their leaders to see what would make them happy and break the famine. They said they wanted to kill seven of Saul's descendants (II Samuel 21:6). David gave them my two half brothers and my five nephews that I had raised (II Samuel 21:8).

KH: How did that make you feel?

Michal: Oh...I knew it had to be done...but I was pretty bitter.

KH: At who?

Michal: Well, at Joshua for not seeking God's face and for sparing the Gibeonites (Joshua 9:14), at Dad for not honoring the treaty, and at David for saving my crippled nephew Mephibosheth and offering the nephews that I had raised instead. I guess I was also bitter at God for this entire situation.

KH: Does David ever come see you?

Michal: Oh, he is friendly to me and always provides for me, but he never spends the night with me. I have no children of my own. That is pretty bad for women in my culture (Genesis 15:2; I Samuel 1:2-18; II Samuel 6:23). So here I sit in this big house full of laughter and eat alone and cry.

KH: Wow! That's quite a story! Can't you go apologize to David for feeling bitter toward him and try to get right with God?

Michal: I have thought of doing that thousands of times. I don't know why I can't bring myself to do it.

KH: David sinned plenty of times. His sin with Bathsheba and the murder of her husband were terrible sins (II Samuel 11), but he knew how to repent and keep his heart right with God (II Samuel 12:13; I Kings 15:3-5; Psalm 32:1-5; 51). God restored his joy (Psalm 51:12). You could have your joy restored, too.

Hey, I'm going in to play with the kids. I wish you would join us.

Michal: Maybe someday. Not now. Good-bye.

KH: Lord, did she ever get her heart right and get rid of that bitterness?

GOD: No, Son. I kept waiting for her, but she did not. Bad things happen to all people. Some get bitter and some get better. She was one who chose to get bitter.

You have poured concrete many times, Son. First you set the forms where you want it to go, then you pour the concrete in and wait for it to set up.

In the same way, you need to set your affection on things above (Colossians 3:2). You can make your heart go where you choose. You can choose to love those who are not very lovely. Michal set her mind on all the negative and chose to get bitter. She wasted her life, Son. Don't do that.

Son, I know some things have happened to you that are unjust. Don't let anyone or anything rob you of your joy. I'll fix the injustices when this mission is over. Keep your eyes on Me, Son. I don't make mistakes and I've got your back.

QUESTIONS FROM THE BIOLOGY TEXTBOOK
December 22nd 2007

KH: Hello. I'm Kent Hovind. Are you the Textbook Author?

Text Book Author (TA): Yes, I am. How can I help you?

KH: I am reading through your biology book and I have a few questions. Do you have time?

TA: Sure, go ahead.

KH: How long have you been teaching biology?

TA: Almost thirty years now.

KH: Your textbook is beautiful and huge—over 1,200 pages!

TA: Thank you. A lot of people worked on it with me. Nearly two hundred people reviewed it for accuracy. We think it is one of the best on the market today.

KH: I taught biology myself for fifteen years.

TA: That's great! We need today's students to learn biology.

KH: I agree. I really enjoyed your opening articles about "How Geckos Defy Gravity" (p. 1). That was an ingenious experiment they designed to measure the weight a gecko could carry on its back while stuck to a ceiling.

TA: I know. The results were staggering! A tiny gecko "could theoretically carry a ninety-pound backpack" (p. 2).

KH: It is amazing, but you finished by saying, "talk about being over-engineered." Do you really believe that the foot of the gecko is "engineered"? The rest of your book dogmatically teaches the evolution theory with no designer.

TA: The "engineered" statement is just a figure of speech. It appears to be engineered but all scientists know that it evolved. There is no designer.

KH: Can you explain why or how a gecko could evolve such an unbelievable "over-engineered" foot like this? I can't imagine how this could happen.

TA: It does seem unbelievable but geckos have it—so it must have evolved. Once we get more grant money, we will do experiments to try to figure out how it evolved. That's the beauty of science. We are always learning (II Timothy 3:7).

KH: Is it possible that it really was engineered?

TA: Oh, NO! That would imply a "designer" and all scientists know that there was not a designer. We can explain everything in the universe with the glorious theory of evolution.

KH: I noticed you start the book by saying that biology is "the scientific study of living organisms and how they have evolved" (p. 3). Isn't there a serious step in the scientific process you are missing?

TA: What step is that?

KH: The obvious first question. Before you study "how they evolved," wouldn't it be logical to determine "if they evolved"? You start with an obvious prejudice.

TA: Oh, NO! All scientists know everything evolved. Now we just need to determine how it happened.

KH: I noticed that you state that "critics outside of science" call evolution "just a theory" (p. 8). Are there any people "inside of science" who don't believe evolution?

TA: Absolutely not! You can't be a scientist and not believe in evolution.

KH: OK, let me see if I have this right. Anyone who does not believe in evolution is not allowed to be called a scientist; therefore, all scientists believe in evolution. Is that the way it is?

TA: Exactly! I couldn't have said it better myself.

KH: What do you mean by the word "evolution"?

TA: Evolution is change over time which applies to all living things (p. 10).

KH: That seems rather vague. Are there limits to the "change"?

TA: Not that we know of. Given enough time, anything can happen. Simple life forms like bacteria can evolve into whales—over millions of years, of course.

KH: Has anyone ever seen a bacteria produce anything other than a bacteria?

TA: No, but it happened about 600 million years ago in the Cambrian era. No one has been able to make it happen today.

KH: In discussing the scientific method, your book says, "When an important discovery is announced in a paper, other scientists attempt to reproduce the result, providing a check on accuracy and honesty. Non-reproducible results are not taken seriously for long" (p. 9).

If no one has been able to reproduce the results of the bacteria story, why should anyone take seriously the idea that it happened 600 million years ago, and only one time? Does that make the bacteria-to-whale idea more religion than science?

TA: Oh, NO! We don't allow religion in the textbooks—only science.

KH: Well, I really don't understand. Your book says, "The scientific process involves the rejection of hypotheses that are inconsistent with experimental results or observations" (p. 9). Yet there have been no experimental results or "observations" of a bacteria producing anything other than a bacteria, so how can the bacteria-to-whale hypothesis not be rejected?

TA: Simple. We don't call it a hypothesis. We call it a fact! That way we don't have to bother explaining that step. Anyone who questions the fact is fired, ridiculed, or banned from publishing in science journals—or all of the above. True science must be protected from pseudo-science these days.

KH: It sounds like you are dedicated to protecting evolution—e-r-r-r, I mean science.

TA: Oh...I am! Our whole team is. That's why we wrote the book.

KH: I must admit that there is an enormous amount of great science in your book.

TA: Thanks, we worked hard on that.

KH: May I ask a few more questions?

TA: Sure. Science has nearly all the answers.

KH: Page 10 of your book has a huge picture of Charles Darwin, by far the largest picture of any individual in the book. Under the picture you call him "the great biologist."

TA: Yes, he was a great biologist and deserves a place of prominence in our book and in history. Doesn't he look grand in that picture?

KH: Yes he does, but I'm curious why you call him a "scientist" when his only degree was in theology. Why don't you call him "Reverend Darwin"?

TA: We don't want to confuse the students. We know he didn't have a science degree, but he did good science research.

KH: Can a person have a theology degree today and still be considered a scientist?

TA: Not unless he also believes in evolution. All scientists believe in evolution.

KH: I see. On page 10 you mention "to this day many people believe in creation."

TA: Yes, can you believe that even in spite of all the advances in science, there are still millions of uneducated people who refuse to see the truth of evolution and hold to "creationism"! We need more money for education. Our school system is failing somehow to get the point across.

KH: Many surveys show that between fifty and sixty percent of the public believes that the earth is only a few thousand years old and God created it.

TA: I know! That energizes me to go work harder to spread the evolution theory!

KH: You said on page 10 that people in Darwin's day thought that species were "specially created and unchangeable, or immutable, over the course of time." This seems a little unfair. Why do you use the word "species" and not the word "kind" as most of them would have used? They all agreed that variations happen within limits. They just didn't think the observed variation could change any plant or animal into a different "kind."

TA: I know I'm slightly misrepresenting their position, but I have to do that so my students will get the point.

KH: What's the point?

TA: That creationists are fools. That creationists are anti-science. That evolution is true!

KH: I think we need to better define that word "evolution." You said, "Darwin's theory of evolution explains and describes how organisms on earth have changed over time and acquired a diversity of new forms" (p. 10). It looks like you have missed several giant steps in the scientific process here.

TA: What steps are those?

KH: You skipped over explaining where the organisms came from. Your theory sort of starts in the middle and takes the origin of time, space, matter, laws, and life for granted.

TA: None of those are really part of science.

KH: Then why do you have an entire chapter, chapter 4, on the topic? Is the origin of life part of evolution theory?

TA: Obviously life had to get started in order to evolve.

KH: I notice on page 60 you say "The consensus among researchers is that life arose spontaneously from these early waters less than four billion years ago." You briefly mention Louis Pasteur on page 56 and page 1152 but never mention his or Redi's experiments showing that spontaneous generation is impossible. Since no one has come close to creating life and this hypothesis is a "non-reproducible result," why would you lead students to believe that the origin of life is even part of science?

TA: We know there are serious problems with spontaneous generation, but we certainly don't want to confuse the students. We feel it is best to gloss over the problems and lead them to believe that future evolutionists can solve these problems as they discover them. Later, in grad school, they can get government grants to do their own research if they like.

KH: I need to go now, but I'd like to ask more questions later if you don't mind.

TA: No problem. Science has solved many problems and I'm confident it can solve many more problems without having to resort to the unscientific "creator" idea. It's actually quite liberating to feel that we evolved and are now masters of our own destiny!

KH: I'm sure it is. I'll get with you later, TA.

AHITHOPHEL
December 24th 2007
(based on 2 Samuel 11:3; 15:12-34; 16:15-23; 17:1-23; 23:34)

KH: Excuse me, Mr. Ahithophel (at II Samuel 17:23), what are you doing with that rope around your neck? It looks like you are going to hang yourself.

Ahithophel (AH): I am.

KH: Why?

AH: It's a long complicated story.

KH: I'd love to hear it.

AH: Well, I'm from Giloh, a city of Judah (Joshua 15:51; II Samuel 15:12). I'm one of King David's counselors and advisors. I'm also a priest of the Lord and always raised my children to fear and obey the Lord.

My son, Eliam, is one of King David's mighty men (II Samuel 23:34). He has been a loyal servant of the king for years. Another of David's might men was a foreigner, a Hittite named Uriah (II Samuel 11:3; 23:39).

My son has a beautiful daughter named Bathsheba. She and Uriah were married several years ago. He was the perfect husband for my granddaughter. He was also a leader of men (II Samuel 11:2).

KH: I've heard that your granddaughter was very beautiful (II Samuel 11:2).

AH: Yes, she was and she knew it. One evening several years ago she was taking a bath and didn't close the curtains. I think she did it on purpose. She knew the king's palace was next door and anyone of the rooftop could see right into her bathroom.

KH: Why do so many beautiful women feel like they should flaunt their bodies and tempt men to lust (Matthew 5:18; I Timothy 2:9)?

AH: I don't know, but she wasn't raised that way! Anyway, her husband was off fighting the enemy. The king should have been with his troops (II Samuel 11:1) but he stayed home and lounged around in bed all day (II Samuel 11:2). When he finally got up and went for a walk on his roof, he saw my granddaughter taking a bath. Instead of turning away like he should have (Matthew 5:28) he watched her bathe and lusted after her (Exodus 20:17 and sent his servants to bring her to the palace. Since she didn't resist or cry out I can only conclude she had a part in all this (Deuteronomy 22:23-27). After their one night fling, she became pregnant. It makes me angry just thinking about it!

KH: Angry at who?

AH: Lots of people. I'm angry at the king for not being where he was supposed to be and for committing adultery with my granddaughter. I'm angry at her for enticing the king like that. I'm angry at the kings messengers for allowing and even helping this sin to take place right in the palace (II Samuel 11:4). They had to know what was going on. Why would anyone assist someone in sin?

KH: Political leaders have done this for centuries and seem to have no problem finding willing assistants. Adolf Hitler had several million help him.

AH: Who?

KH: Ah...never mind. I'll explain later. I still don't understand why you need to hang yourself.

AH: Well...when David found out Bathsheba was pregnant he had my son in law, Uriah killed and quickly married Bathsheba to cover up his sin. Everyone thought the baby was his.

KH: Boy! This all sounds like the Maury Povich television show!

AH: The what?

KH: Ah...never mind, that would really take a long time to explain! So what happened after David married your granddaughter? Were you working as David's counselor all this time?

AH: Yes, I was and it was real hard to even be near him knowing all the secrets he was hiding. Boy, those politicians are real good at hiding all the skeletons in their closets!

KH: That's for sure! Nothing has changed.

AH: Anyway, God sent the prophet Nathan to expose David's sin (II Samuel 12:1-12) and four real bad things happened to David (II Samuel 12-18). I'm here now, ready to hang myself because of the fourth one.

KH: I still don't understand. If God is judging David's sin, why would you need to hang yourself? It seems like David aught to be hanged.

AH: Oh, I agree! And that's the problem. When David's son Absalom rebelled against his dad, he sent for me to work for him as counselor (II Samuel 15:12); so I took the job.

KH: Had David repented of his sin?

AH: Yes, very sincerely (Psalm 51).

KH: Did God forgive him?

AH: Yes (II Samuel 12:13).

KH: Did you forgive David?

AH: No, and that's part of why I must kill myself. I've been harboring bitterness in my heart for a long time now.

KH: I don't get it. David and Bathsheba's baby died (II Samuel 12:19), David's son Amnon raped his half sister, Tamar (II Samuel 13), Absalom killed Amnon (II Samuel 13:21-29), and now Absalom is leading a rebellion against his own dad. Hasn't David paid enough?

AH: Maybe in God's eyes, but not in mine.

KH: Don't David and Bathsheba have another baby now?

AH: Yes, Solomon (II Samuel 12:24). He will never amount to anything. God can't possibly use a child from that unholy union.

KH: Oh, you might be surprised. God can use anyone! You shouldn't have bitterness toward your own great-grandson. He didn't do anything wrong. By the way, aren't you a descendant of Judah?

AH: Yes I am.

KH: Didn't Judah have an illicit relation with his own daughter-in-law to produce your ancestor (Genesis 38)?

AH: Yes, but that's different.

KH: I don't see how. It's amazing how people can preach hard against other's sins yet not see it in themselves! If God forgives, we should too. I still don't see why you think suicide is the only answer.

AH: Because Absalom is going to lose the battle tomorrow and I will be hanged for treason.

KH: How do you know Absalom will lose?

AH: I gave him sound advice on how to defeat David (II Samuel 17:1-4) and even offered to lead the attack, but Absalom chose to follow the advice of Hushai instead. It won't work. All it does is give David time to escape and rest up. I've given counsel for years. I'm sure he will lose.

KH: If you offered to lead the attack at your age, you must really be carrying a grudge!

AH: I am. It eats at me every day.

KH: Yes, grudges do that. Say, you give counsel to lots of people as a priest. Why don't you analyze exactly who you are angry with.

AH: OK. Let's see…I'm angry at Bathsheba for seducing the king. I'm angry at David for not being where he should have been and for committing adultery with my granddaughter. I'm angry at Absalom for being too dumb to see that he is following bad advice. And, I'm angry at myself for allowing all this to happen.

KH: I think you missed the main one.

AH: Who is that?

KH: God. That's really where your problem lies.

AH: Yes. I'm angry at God for forgiving David and Bathsheba. It's just not right.

KH: I really think you are looking at this all wrong. You offer sacrifices (II Samuel 15:12) for people. You, of all people, should know that God is a God of mercy, slow to anger, and of great kindness (Jonah 4:2). Your anger sounds like the anger of Jonah. He got angry because God forgave sin as well.

I really think you should take that rope off your neck and get down here on your knees and ask God to help you get the bitterness out of your heart. Then, go talk with David and work out your differences. He understands forgiveness really well.

I also think you should accept that new great-grandson, Solomon and help him grow up. You might be surprised at how God can use our mistakes and failures for His glory.

AH: No. My mind is made up. Ahhhhhhhh!

KH: No, Ahithophel! Why did you jump?

Kent Hovind leaves Ahithophel

KH: God, how many people have killed themselves like this rather than accept your free forgiveness?

GOD: You wouldn't believe Me if I told you, Son. If only people could learn to trust Me and accept My forgiveness for themselves and others, this world would be a much better place.

KH: Lord, are there some people I know following Ahithophel's path?

GOD: Yes, Son, there are. Here, I'll hold your hand and we'll go find some.

KH: Thanks, Lord. You are awesome!

GOD: I know, Son. I've got your back.

2007 END OF THE YEAR UPDATE
December 31st 2007

Wow! What a year! God has been so good! The ministry is still going well. I'm still in prison in South Carolina, but God is able to get me out at a moment's notice (Acts 12:5). The Motion for Release Pending Appeal was filed December 20th and we await the decision of the 11th Circuit Court of Appeals. The transcripts are still not finished. Now is the time for concerted, fervent prayer for God to show His mighty power in this case.

As I have done for nearly thirty-nine years, I encourage all of us to read Luke 2:52 this time of year and take stock of our lives in four areas—physical, mental, social, and spiritual. Did we improve in each area last year?

The Lord is due back any minute to take the Christians from the earth. We need to use our limited time left on earth to win souls and influence others for Him. Nothing else will matter in a hundred years!

Blessed New Year!
Kent Hovind